DIARY OF

AN

AIREDALE

DIARY OF

AN

AIREDALE

a terrier's tale

Volume IV

Also by

P. J. Erickson

Yokche
The Nature of Murder

Kill Devil
Mystery of the Cane

for Maggie

"Live. Laugh. Bark."

- Unknown

ACKNOWLEDGEMENTS

My heartfelt thanks to everyone who enjoys reading about Alf's antics, and especially to those awesome people who devote their time and resources to rescuing animals in distress.

AUTHOR'S NOTE

Talking dogs are not yet in the realm of believability, so Alf's adventures are creations of my imagination, even though I did extensive research on the information sprinkled throughout the book.

That said, neither Alf nor I are experts in any of these subjects. It is our hope that you will discover something new and want to learn more, but please be sure to check things out for yourself. This is, after all, a work of fiction.

I hope you enjoy this fourth foray into the life of Alf Airedale and thank you for your interest.

- P. J. Erickson

Table of Contents

A barking rad birthday..*3*

Aireborne..*17*

Hot Aire *37*

SuperDale..*57*

Howloween *73*

Aire travel *87*

Thankswoofing Outing *103*

Merry Woofmas *109*

Aire dysfunction..*121*

Aire attack *127*

Aire cooled..*135*

Airebrushed *139*

Dire times..*143*

Aire horn *147*

A bridge too far..*159*

HI FOLKS. ALF HERE. Yes, it's that time again. Have you missed me? I am truly humbled by your interest. I trust you are dumbstruck by that statement since humble is not a word in our language, but in this case, I admit, yes I am.

My birthday is barreling down the days faster than a squirrel with me on its heels. I am more handsome than ever of course, still fun-loving and energetic. I've seen lots of pictures on Anna's screen thing this year of some of you having such interesting times — running free in the woods, swimming in the streams, chasing sticks, wow. Can't do that here because of those monstrous gray scaly things. Then some of you live in the country with horses, goats, pigs, and even cats. I'd love that. I saw all that white cold stuff too. *How cool.* My life is not nearly as exciting but I've still got a story to tell, so I hope you'll join me again for the ride through my next year. Here we go, another trip into Aireland.

A barking rad birthday

YAPPY BARKDAY TO ME, *WOOFS*. We celebrated twice this year for my birthday because Father's Day falls on the same day, and, as we all know, Harry is a first-rate fur-kid dad. After breakfast he winked at me and asked,

"Wanna go for a ride Alf?"

Do I? woofs, yips and spins.

"Okay then, go fetch your leash. Just us guys, as it's our special day, yeah?"

"Hold it fellas, not so fast." Anna had been listening and now stood in front of the door. "No fair leaving me out of the fun."

"Just kidding," Harry said as I turned my head back and forth between them like one of

3

those little plastic balls people bounce on a big table."It wouldn't be any fun without you. Hurry and get ready."

I ran around, hounding (get it?) the pawrents, so excited. Harry knows I love car rides and this year he drove to a place we hadn't visited before and stopped in a huge park, *yips*. I spent ages exploring, refusing to continue until I sniffed my fill. To be fair, my people hung out enjoying their slow amble while I did my thing.

Done, I looked around to check everyone's whereabouts, and caught a whiff of the endless water (sea to you) and heard its roar. The park still needed investigation but my folks, finished with their walk wanted to keep going. I confess to a smidgeon of disappointment.

On previous visits to the beach I had been leashed, which took a severe toll on my ability to have a good time. When Harry pulled out a load of gear from the back of the Airemobile and loaded himself up, I glumly expected the same arrangement as I trudged up some wooden stairs behind them. Once on the top, we stood looking over small hills covered with long waving grass. The beach came into view, reaching farther than I could see, which impressed me no end. This beach stretched forever, or perhaps just gave that impression because I could see much farther from my vantage point.

With some reluctance and a yearning gaze back at the park, I followed my leash down to the yellow dirt and waited while the folks dumped all the gear they carried. Perhaps on the way back they'd let me explore a bit more.

A playful breeze blew off the water carrying unfamiliar scents which caused my nose to twitch nonstop. We hadn't visited this beach before, and much to my amazement, we saw no other people. I perked up, perceiving that this place might be a lot more fun, that is until a glance at the folks sent my mood plummeting again. Dejection set in and I stood apart, sniffing the air while the humans arranged their belongings and sat down to relax.

No way. This is a joke, right? We came all this way to stay in one spot? I glimpsed long, tempting stretches with no people. *What a waste.* Bummed out I stayed put, refusing to sit, so upset with this supposed birthday adventure. Miffed with them I presented my family with a view of my butt. You could have bowled me over with a feather when a moment later, Anna startled me by creeping up and unclipping my leash.

Free? I'm allowed to check things out on my own? Alright, that's why Harry brought us here today, just for me. What a guy! Nobody's better than Harry, eh? Free to do whatever I want, I hesitated a moment, to be sure the humans meant to do this, but no, they both shooed me away.

"Go ahead Alf, have fun."

I awarded them my biggest grin then took off running, looking back only once to see if they were checking up on me. Satisfied they weren't, I raced around all over the place before slowing to an amble so I could wander around for a more detailed investigation.

I found some odd-looking brownish weed, giving off such an enticing stench I couldn't resist wallowing in it, soaking myself in its heavenly stink. Satisfied with my wondrous new perfume I took a few moments to rest and delight in my new discovery before my brain kicked in and it occurred to me, too late, I had committed a no-no.

Oh oh. I risked a quick, guilty glance at my humans, relieved to see them otherwise engaged. *Whew.* I raced along the hard-packed brown stuff, beating a hasty retreat with my tail tucked when the water surged in trying to reach me. I'm not fond of the wet stuff, especially when it seems to have a life of its own, but the beach, wow, what a wonderful place.

A bit further on I almost stepped on a small deep hole. Leaning down to get a better look, imagine my shock when a freaky creature with arms that ended in monstrous pincers jumped out and rushed toward me. It waved those things in the air, clacking them together as it targeted my nose, which, as we all know is of goodly size.

This small creature bobbed and weaved like a boxer, thrusting up those fearsome weapons with admirable aggressiveness. The thought of them grabbing my nose made me shudder. I'm proud of my gorgeous schnoz and safeguarded it with the instant activation of my lightning reflexes. That's an Airedale trait.

I'd seen a creature like this once before, as you may remember, but this one moved so fast I didn't recognize it. I warily kept a safe distance from those vicious pincers suspecting they could deliver an agonizing crunch if they managed to grab a piece of me.

Out of the corner of my eye I glimpsed Anna laughing at me as she took my picture. Affronted, I pretended bravado as I backed up to a safe distance, with the proper amount of caution, you understand, before making any more inspections.

Imagine my surprise when the critter raced sideways snapping those supersize claws at me, then scuttled away towards the water. I chased after it intrigued but too far away to catch up and it disappeared beneath the water before I made contact. *A mysterious place, this beach.*

Undaunted by this encounter, and damp from the spray, I rolled in the weed stuff again and came up covered in the grainy yellow dirt with pieces of brown weed stuck in my hair like long curls. How wonderful it felt, with no people slowing me down or giving me orders. It doesn't get any better than this for us four-legged guys.

Continuing my research I nosed a few shells, chose one with a spectacular tangy aroma and picked it up, tearing towards the tall grass on the higher ground, throwing and catching my new treasure as I went. Weaving through the grass and the small hillocks it grew on, nothing caught my attention. The sand, paler up here, made it difficult to walk through. It looked like the sugar stuff I wasn't allowed to eat and scorched my paws. Losing interest and with my belly starting to rumble, I began to saunter back to my people. Perhaps they brought food. All this snuffling is quite tiring for us guys. I trotted up, almost to the chairs, when they both glanced up and yelled at me at the same time.

"Alffffffffffff."

What? Is someone chasing me? Stunned I sat on my haunches. *Were they in danger of some sort? Had something happened when I abandoned my guard dog duties for play?* They both got up and came to me, Anna holding her nose as she did. *Oh is that all? She didn't like my lovely aroma?* Harry put his hands on his hips but broke out in guffaws when I stared at him, tilting my head in question. No subtlety here. People require obvious signals to be able to understand.

"You are a sight my boy. Wish I brought my phone. This would be a picture for posterity." He stretched out a hand to rub my head but then thought better of it.

I switched my gaze to Anna who looked me up and down and shook her head then pulled the leash from behind her back. "Well, you certainly had a fine time didn't you Alf? I'm so glad, but in the state you're in you can't get in the car. It's the showers for you my lad."

The dreaded shower, on my birthday. People sure knew how to ruin the best day in ages. What's wrong with my state? I smell terrific. I backed up a bit and gave Anna my most appealing sorrowful face.

"None of that Alf, it won't work this time. Come along."

Nope. Not happening.

My humans had not yet experienced Airedale stubbornness, but they would now. I planted my feet and braced myself, confident the immoveable quality of my pose would hold, but I proved to be no match for my favorite people. Anna pulled while Harry pushed and I dragged my butt, alas to no avail.

We arrived at the dreaded shower and before a protest could reach my mouth, I found myself under a torrent of warmish water, shocked into submission. Outraged I put all my energy into the biggest, best shake ever performed, which drenched Anna and Harry while I watched with my smuggest expression.

Two young humans who picked that exact moment to walk past, were also gifted with my wrath. Pleased with myself I grinned up at my audience but snapped my mouth shut in a hurry as another deluge soaked me once again. I should have known better than to try and scam Harry because when the doggone bath finally stopped, a humungous towel landed on me, threatening suffocation, and Harry started rubbing me dry, none too gently.

Anna, always the soft touch, took pity on me. "Much better Alf." She gave me a smooch and I forgave her. Wasn't ready to forgive Harry just yet though. "Now you're presentable, how about some ice cream?"

Ice cream, yeah, my favorite. All is forgiven. I pummeled Harry with my tail in thanks and walked about in impatient circles while the folks packed our things in the car. At last I jumped in and we took off. If my birthday stopped now, it had been a blast and a half, quite the best day in ages. Harry, holding his nose and breathing through his mouth, opened the windows to let out the smell of wet dog. So he said. Can't think why. I've always liked that particular Aireoma myself but I admitted it helped to finish drying me off so when we arrived at the ice cream shop I passed as presentable.

My mouth watered while we stood in line and I couldn't stop wriggling in anticipation. I stood up, and put my paws on the counter, to make sure Harry ordered the right amount and also to eyeball all the goodies on display.

The lady behind the counter grinned at me as she asked, "What can I do for you young fella?" I returned the grin and tried to lick her hand to check for available flavors but of course, Harry intervened.

"Alf likes vanilla cones best," he told her.

"Coming right up," she said, scratching my throat while Harry searched for his money. My eyes grew bigger than my favorite ball when the lady handed him a cone so whopping it filled my vision and for just a few seconds, grave doubts surfaced about my ability to handle it. This must be the origin of the human saying, 'his mouth is bigger than his stomach.'

Deciding this was not the case I sidled up to Harry, trying to figure out the best approach to this wondrous concoction. Harry held it for me while I channeled my best slurp, determined not to let one drop melt before my tongue reached it.

A couple of kids seated nearby with their family went into fits of giggles watching my heroic attempts not to miss a drop, but they waited until I finished before bounding over to say hello. I'd long forgotten the horrid little boy who tormented me when I was a young pup and though I didn't come into contact with the little people often, I loved playing with them because their energy equaled mine. Sometimes I forgot myself and got a bit too rough in my excitement but these two boys proved to be no strangers to roughness. We all had a blast in a fenced area next to the tables and chairs, wrestling and chasing a ball until their parents got ready to leave. Good thing too. I didn't want to admit to being pooped when they showed no sign of flagging. As a thank you for playing with me, I sat between them wearing my biggest smile while the people took our picture.

Back home we left Anna to her own devices while Harry and I settled into our comfy sofa for an extended snooze. Awesome day. Oh, I almost forgot, dinner turned out to be liver and birthday cake. How could I forget that? Anna spent ages making it, under my watchful scrutiny, meaning I tried to put my nose into everything. My cake. I had to approve didn't I?

"Okay Alf. You're title is chief taster after all. Is it okay so far?"

Yep, it certainly is. Busy licking the bowl Anna proffered I gave her an enthusiastic tails up. I supervised as she poured the stuff into her bowl, peanut butter, pumpkin, carrot, yogurt and apple. *Yum.* My mouth watered even more when she put it into the hot box to cook and all the whiffs of something delicious wafted out and filled the house. The liver melted in my mouth but when she put the cake down in front of me, *wowzer.* Why the folks didn't want any was beyond me. I offered to share. Silly people, all the more for me, and that wasn't all.

Sated with food, my belly full, I became quite dozy and needed a nap, but waddling to my bed I stopped in my tracks when Anna brought out the best gift of all, a teddy baire. My people did me royal on my birthday, outdoing themselves. I've always known they love me and I am family, but today left me almost incoherent with love for them. That said, that baire waited, my size, honey colored like me and furry. I gave it a good sniff, then gently accepted it with suppressed glee.

I had, for a while now, become intrigued by girls and being an only fur-kid had no one to go to for information on the subject, but now I had Teddie and I could practice, and practice I did, every night, much to Anna's dismay.

She banned Teddie, carrying her to the back room of the house with me following on her heels in protective mode. Every evening after dinner I rushed back there to work on perfecting my technique. They didn't know it, a dog must have some secrets you know, but at the last meet with my pals, a buddy and I wandered off with one of the girls and discovered the delights of female company. No one spotted us to warn us off and I left eager to continue at the next meeting. My name is Alf but Harry and Anna often call me No, or Leave it. I'm jake with that.

P. J. Erickson

·

Aireborne

THIS MONTH BARRELED IN with unbaireable heat and humidity. I'm not a fan of heat so spent most of my time indoors, only venturing out early in the morning and late in the evening. Some days have brought warm zippy breezes which help with the heat a bit, at least keep those hateful little flying bugs at bay, but still, no fun.

The folks bought me a travel home for when we go on trips. I don't know why they thought that was a good idea, but, oh well. It's a crate with a mesh door and cloth sides. They added a thick comfy pad for the floor. I ventured over to investigate but I don't like small spaces and it didn't smell right. Also, I don't want to give them the idea I'm easy to please so I gave it a desultory nose poke and declined to go near it. Anna tried to bribe me my dropping treats inside but I only snuck in far enough to grab the treat when they weren't looking. After a couple of weeks she gave up trying and I continued to enjoy my snug fluffy bed in peace.

I spent so much time lazing on the couch, despite Anna's efforts to amuse me, that I got quite interested in the TV. Yes, I finally learned the name of the moving picture frame. Did you know the average pooch now eyeballs about nine hours of TV a week? Yes, and here's something I bet you didn't know- some genius somewhere created a remote control for us dogs. Cross my heart, well, my paws anyway.

An English researcher and a pet food outfit created it. It's blue and yellow for our eyesight. The buttons are oversized and each one gives off a different sound when pushed. They say it's chew proof but Anna will have to buy one for me to verify it's Airedale proof, and get this, the channel button is bone shaped, the play button is a ball and the pause button is, guess what, a paw print of course. Anna snuck a gander at me from the side of her eye while she read this.

Catching me looking, she waggled her finger. "No chance Alf, you'd change channels every few seconds, never mind the noise."

Spoilsport. Sometimes my humans are too dull, no sense of adventure. Oh well, perhaps someday some kind soul might send me one. The way they talked sometimes you would think I am the Prince of Darkness. *Hmph.*

One day, watching a program with Anna I learned that a man named Pablo Picasso shared his home with an Airedale called Elf back around 1930. That's beyond my ability to calculate in dog years, so I was keen to have a gander at this fella. Elf, Alf, almost kindred spirits eh?

Anna told me this man used a brush dipped in colors to make pictures on blank paper. People, it seemed, were more drawn to those than to his fur-kid. I sat up to eyeball some of his paintings expecting to see at least one of Elf, but all that happened was that Anna almost fell off her chair laughing at how many head tilts I did. I tried looking at them upside down but I still saw a picture full of blue splotches, certainly no one called Elf, so disappointing. At that point I lost interest and went back to my bed.

As the days progressed, still with unrelenting heat, I grew ever more lazy and bored until one day Anna asked "Alf, how would you like to go to Dogwarts?"

I threw her one of my, *not on your life*, smirks. It didn't sound like something on my list of rad things to do, so I turned my head and gave her my side-eye look. I'm sure you know the one.

Interpreting my response, Anna chuckled. "No need to panic Alf, Dogwarts is going to be our wizarding school, you know like Hogwarts. You watched that Harry Potter movie with me, remember?"

Oh, yes I did remember that movie. It had all kinds of fascinating creatures in it. Was Anna going to work magic like having treats appear out of nowhere? She had my attention now, even more so when she jumped up, rearranged some furniture and came back with not one but several treats all with different flavors. I trotted over, nose targeted on the tastiest treat, liver if my smeller hadn't failed me and it never did. Yes, I've been called nosy. *Okay, I'm in. What do we do?*

By the way, did you know that perfect as we are, Airedales are prone to nose cancer, perish the thought. Why are we talking about this now? I thought I heard you ask. You told us this before when you met poor Buttons, the Irish Setter. I understand I threw you off track but I am the Einstein of Airedales after all and this is something you need in your arsenal of doggy lore. The welfare of my brothers and sisters is all important to me and I have valuable information here. This particular nasty happens, in most cases, to older dogs but can occur at any time, and did, to my pal Boomer. It was terrible to see him suffering with this awful thing which is why I'm telling you about it again.

Keep an eye out for a runny nose and while it may clear with treatment, don't let your guard down because you didn't get a diagnosis. The discharge may be bloody, clear or like mucus and often comes from one side of the nose. As the tumor grows it may begin to emerge from both sides and your furkid may start sneezing or making snoring sounds. If it grows big enough it can cause the face to appear deformed and destroy surrounding soft and bony tissue. So you can tell this is nothing to sneeze about eh? *Okay, okay, sorry for the pun, not funny.* To make matters worse, it may spread to the brain and cause, among other things, behavior changes, blindness or even seizures. Symptoms can mimic other conditions which might delay a proper diagnosis. Those of us with long noses are at higher risk and if we are exposed to tobacco smoke and other airborne pollutants the risk increases.

The people who study this stuff found some connection of nasal tumors with flea spray, so keep that in mind. Diagnosis is made through scans, biopsies and bone pictures though because symptoms are often masked, the condition may not be recognized until it is too advanced and surgery not possible. Treatment is the same as for people cancers, with radiation and chemotherapy, which can result in remission.

There is more unpleasant information about this condition but I've given you the gist of it so you will be aware of what to watch for, and only because, I'm sad to say, we Airedales do have a predisposition to this dreadful disease. Sorry for ruining the mood. I do get distracted, so let's get back to business.

Well Dogwarts wasn't exactly magic but we both got a kick from it. Every day from then on

Anna taught me a new trick. I am the possessor of a brilliant mind, as by now you are aware, so I scored lots of rewards and Anna started to worry I would put on too much weight. We played three different games at intervals during the day. They didn't last long but we both had fun and I found using my noggin to figure things out took about as much stamina as running around. Win, win for everyone and boredom gone.

My people are the best. My favorite game is 'find it'. She would hide toys, sometimes food and sometimes she hid herself. This last one is so much fun I turned the tables on her. I would steal a shoe or maybe a sock and hide it then demand the folks go search for it, or sometimes I would hide when they called me. Turns out my people didn't much like this turn of events. What party poopers. I only wanted to tempt them to have as much fun as I had. People need more fun. They don't take enough time to play. Sad.

Then, one boring evening, while dozing on the sofa for lack of anything else to do, trying to block out Harry's voice droning into his phone, my ears tuned into the magic words, "yes, we're leaving tomorrow."

Leaving? Where? Me too?

"No." Harry said, "I have to find a boarding place that will take Alf."

What? Banished to an Aire BnB? No way.

I snuck up to Harry and laid my head on his knee, tail wagging in appeal, devastated at the thought of being left behind. A few minutes later, while absently stroking my ears, Harry finished his talk. He glanced down at me with a grin. "Ease up Alf. What would a trip be without you? Of course you are coming with us. I just couldn't resist a chance to yank your tail."

I sprang up and fixed him with my fiercest stare. Harry had a weird sense of humor but this prank crossed the line and it cut me to the quick. Harry ought to be ashamed of himself. I don't always make my displeasure known, but when I do, best watch out. However payback must wait. I needed to prepare for travel.

Early the next morning we hit the road, and stayed on it all day. I spent my time snoozing, not liking the motion at high speeds but when the motion slowed I opened one eye to check on our whereabouts. Harry slowed the car, unsure of the direction. We had been traveling on boring roads with not much in sight except for the occasional rusted out gas station and a grass bale or two, which interested me but did nothing to excite the human travelers.

Harry's patience started to work itself into frustration. "Are you sure we're going the right way?" He asked Anna.

"Yes. It's not too far now."

"We're in the middle of nowhere. This can't be it." Harry complained.

The tension between the folks rose and I got a little anxious as we continued in silence. I sensed Harry was about to lose his cool. He had been driving for many hours and we were all a bit frazzled, but just then Anna said "turn left here."

Harry did as ordered and and we all stared in amazement. The countryside now consisted of steep hills studded with leafy green trees, not the tall palms we grew at home. The sudden change from the flat, desolate road we left seconds ago left us breathless. We traveled for some time, up and down these hills until we came to a built-up area and Harry pulled into a side road in front of a long building, not new like most of the houses we passed on the way, but well-cared for. This hotel took up a humungous piece of ground, not tall but spread out and separated into different human kennels. We all piled out of the car and after Harry checked in, I trailed after them until they found our room in a smaller building on the side. The folks beamed with delight as they walked in, exclaiming over this and that as they explored. I performed my mandatory inspection, finding a homey type room with an oversized bathroom. Everything looked a bit old-fashioned, historic, Anna called it, although clean and colorful and appeared to be what they expected.

We all collapsed, beat after traveling so long. I expected to be fed and left while they went in search of dinner, but no, we all went. The streets in the town were hilly too and all along them we spotted intriguing-looking stores and restaurants. I lagged behind, trying to take it all in, but the folks grumped, wanting dinner and bed, so I didn't learn much as we stopped at the first place we found.

A big wall hid it from view but once inside the door we discovered an outdoor area scattered with tables and chairs, shaded by those gaudy umbrella things, where the waitress welcomed me to sit for dinner with the humans. We all decided on fish and chips. Only two portions of course, but I scored my share from both of them, *yum*, and the owners brought me a bowl of water almost big enough to paddle in.

The other diners all came over to meet me. I figured Airedales must be rare in this town but I took the homage as my due and was polite, even though they were rudely interrupting my meal. I scored more delicious tidbits with my gracious cuteness until caught red-pawed. Full and sleepy, I didn't mind the scolding, happy by then to go back to our room and settle in.

Unbeknownst to me, Anna brought my travel crate, you remember, the one I refused to use, and I did so now as payback to Harry. An Airedale never forgets. Instead I jumped on the pawrents' comfy bed and pretended to settle for the night. After a while I jumped down and stretched out on the lovely cold tile in the bathroom and bid everyone goodnight. Anna shrugged, too weary to be bothered and she and Harry both turned in.

Early the next morning we were up and at 'em, traveling to an enormous field, covered in little white tents where people stood selling stuff.

I got to investigate all the goods with my people. We even found several places selling things for me, gear like bandanas and leashes, and best of all food and treats. I like this town. It is a most dog friendly place. After the folks finished lunch we returned to the human kennel and I lapsed into a relaxed sense of contentment, not taking much notice as we walked on a long path behind the rooms. It ended at one made of wood strips which stretched across the top of the lake. It is quite an understatement to tell you that nothing prepared me for the next adventure.

We stopped at a booth where Harry bought tickets and when we turned around, *yikes*, parked right there in front of me sat one of those flying monsters which brought me and Anna to our home all those years ago.

That terrifying experience imprinted itself on my brain. I flagged it as a 'never again' moment with my fervent wish to never set eyes on another one of those things. My hope shattered, I emerged from my shock long enough to realize this monster was tiny in comparison with only room for two or three people and it sat on the water. I didn't care. The Airebrakes activated and

I balked, refusing to move. To make sure they understood I flopped on my side and presented my best stink-eye. *No, no and no, no chance, not happening, uh uh.*

Harry ignored my protest, took my leash and tugged it so I would stand up. I didn't. I stayed put. Harry dragged me along, used to my pranks, perhaps believing this a new one of my jokes. People passing by stared and laughed. A few even made joking remarks and some of the ladies threw angry stares and muttered about cruelty to animals. I made the most of these comments, working my pitiful, abused routine to the max.

Harry took no notice and didn't stop but he did get upset about being embarrassed this way and joked with the people, trying to make light of the situation.

"See Harry," Anna said, taking my leash from him. "I told you. It's cruel to make him get on that thing. I know you've always wanted a ride in a seaplane but you should do this by yourself. Alf and I will stay here and wait for you." I inched closer to Anna knowing she understood the trauma a trip in one of these had caused and would protect me.

Harry sat down on a nearby bench, calling me over. Since this request allowed me to shuffle back, away from the danger, I agreed, against my better judgement, and clambered onto the bench next to him. He put his arm around me, hugging slightly. "Look Alf. It's small and hardly noisy at all, certainly no more than other noises that don't bother you. I really want to do this and I need you to help Anna. She's like you, much happier with her feet on the ground. You're an Airedale, you can do this, no sweat. I think you'll like it too and guess what? Tonight we're going to a fancy eating place for dinner and we'll order a steak and the trimmings all for you.

Oh, and guess what else? There's a plane out there honored with your family name? Yes, an Airedale G ARXB, developed in the 1960s. Sadly they only made a few but I hear some are still left in Australia and New Zealand, and the Doncaster Museum in England has one on display. Wish we could both go and see it, eh? Maybe one day."

I sat up straighter. *Well why didn't you say so?* This changed things. Harry must really want this to offer such a fine bribe, not something he did often, and being Harry he knew exactly which buttons to push. Steak rated top of the list. As a king of terriers I'm obliged to uphold the honor of anything Airedale, even if it scared the hair off me. I found out later my tribe's flying machine's real name was Beagle A 109 Airedale, a bit of an affront with the Beagle name coming first, but Beagle Aircraft made the plane and by then I didn't dwell on it much.

This last bit of information changed things. One of those monsters carried our name and I could earn the right to sink my teeth into a full steak dinner. My reputation and that of my breed hung on the line here. How could I refuse a ride in a machine made for us? I stared into Harry's eyes, checking for the truth, then gazed at the little red and white contraption floating next to the dock. It looked harmless, but things are not always as they seem.

Anna leant against the rail, arms crossed, eyes squinted, watching the exchange between Harry and me. *Alright then. I can do this. I might have the fright of my life and I might be terrified but I would uphold the honor of my relatives.* Anna's mouth dropped open as I got up and trotted by Harry's side towards my destiny. She didn't say anything but hurried after us as Harry said "All right Alf, way to go, thanks boy." Saying this machine was small was a big understatement. Bracing for the inevitable, I spent the time waiting for Anna to climb in debating the merits of a hasty retreat. This event went on for some time as Anna found she needed to make her entrance on her hands and knees crawling doggy-style to reach the back seat. I tried hard not to chuff at the vision of my favorite human in this position, but it took some effort for me to remain dignified. Humans look so silly on all fours.

Anna is a good sport and her determination put me to shame. If Anna could do it. I could too. Watching her inelegant entrance I thought this a suitable way to enter a machine not made for us. I puzzled about why this was so. Airedales don't fly and we are not the fastest dogs on the planet, but mine is not to reason why.

Once inside, Anna managed to turn around and sit behind the pilot, a young fella patiently waiting for us to settle. Then came my turn. With some trepidation I wriggled in next to Anna, relieved to find I didn't have to jump over any water but could step in from the wooden floor.

Harry climbed into the empty front seat and the pilot started the engine. With my eyes like saucers, but otherwise giving no sign of strain, I watched as we started to move, and discovered Harry did not lie. This metal contraption didn't make much noise at all, sort of like the buzz of an annoying insect.

I sat still in my Airespace, stiff as a deer frozen in the headlights. Pretending calm, took every ounce of my Airedale stoicism, but every muscle remained taut as we rushed across the water and into the air. Watching the others out of the corner of my eye, I spied Anna's white fingers clutching the seatback and Harry's focus on the instruments and realized no one paid any interest to my stress level. *Good*. Can't let the tribe down.

The plane sputtered along, not far above the ground and I could gaze out of the window at the land and houses below, not so bad. I relaxed a little, dare I say I even started to enjoy myself, that is until Anna overheard Harry discussing the state of the instruments with the pilot, detailing the less than stellar condition they were in.

Then I stiffened into a stone statue, horrified. *I remembered the time we all rode with Harry in his ancient truck, enjoying the drive until Harry said "Look at this."*

Anna and I both looked in horror at Harry holding the steering wheel in his hands, separated from the long stick it had been attached to. "No worries" Harry said. "Easy to fix."

"No worries my foot." Anna all but yelped. "Are you mad? We could have been killed if that happened on the interstate."

Harry just grinned, enjoying his little jest. Like I said, he has a strange sense of humor sometimes.

Anna and I froze, remembering Harry's lack of concern in situations like this, but he did know what he was talking about because he used to work on aircraft and he stayed informed on new technologies with avid persistence.

I never knew that and now I understood why this trip meant so much to him. He was in his element and I was glad I stepped up to do this with all of us. Anna and I stayed tense for the rest of the flight, but it didn't last long and soon we landed back at the dock.

I jumped out to land on solid ground, pleased with myself. Poor Anna found it more difficult getting out than getting in. I turned back to help her and she grabbed my harness at one point, but she managed an ungainly exit without complaint. Harry chattered nonstop all the way back to the human kennel, still ecstatic. Anna and I grinned at each other like conspirators. We made Harry's day, yes, so cool.

Harry kept his promise. That evening we walked to a fancy-looking restaurant with an outside courtyard, but to reach it we needed to go through the eating room. I didn't hold out much hope that would happen. Dude, was I wrong. The manager, or owner, turned out to be a fun guy. Winking at me he picked up menus and offering us a bow, ushered us out to a small but beautiful yard hidden away by a tall fence and crowded with enough leafy plants to make a mini forest.

The dramatic performance our host gave at our entrance caused a bit of a stir and several people left their tables to come out and meet me. I preened like a movie star as they oohed and aahed and peppered my people with questions. After a few minutes of this, my stomach rumbled and I began to wonder why they made such a fuss. *Had these folk never seen a dog before? What dull lives they must lead.* Fortunately, our meals arrived at last and everyone went back to their own tables. As promised, Harry got me a steak with all the trimmings and I chowed down with gusto. We feasted like kings, a glorious way to finish our little vacation and I hoped we could come back here again one day, minus the flying thing, of course.

On the way out I made sure to stop and thank my new friend, our host, with a raised paw and a couple of licks. Harry and Anna also thanked him, grateful for the kindness in allowing us all to enjoy our dinner in such a fine establishment.

Hot Aire

C AN YOU BELIEVE IT, it's even hotter than last month and muggier too? I'm finding it hard to contain my boredom and not go looking for trouble. Anna is tired of it too. I heard her mutter something about the Dog Days of summer which made me cock my head wondering what she meant. She'd talked about this subject before. Is it a special time for us dogs? If so whichever bright spark thought that up could have done a whole lot better.

It turns out, as I discovered later, this event occurs in an exact period of time, July 3 to August 11 for you humans, the days following the rising of Sirius, the Dog Star. Astrologists connected this time with heat, drought, sudden thunderstorms, sleepiness, fever, mad dogs and bad luck. Why?

Well because Sirius, (so named because it means glowing or scorching,) is the brightest star, nearest to the sun in summer.

Did dogs go nuts only in summer, or did they mean we just got grumpy? I think people behaved badly here giving us noble companions such a bad rap. In any case, what's all this got to do with us dogs?

It turns out a group of stars around Sirius, is called Canis Major because it has the shape of a dog. *Ah, the plot thickens.* This arrangement of stars, according to people, looks like one of the hunting dogs belonging to Orion - you know, one of those Greek guys from long ago, and that's where this whole Dog Days of Summer thing began. Imagine. I'm informed Sirius is either an eye or a nose on this starry dog. Next time we go out at night I'm going to try and find him.These miserable days are now recognized as the hottest, most uncomfortable part of summer.

Bored we were, with the heat keeping us indoors, so the TV stayed on a lot longer during the day. Not happy with any of the offerings, Anna started browsing through different exercise programs and settled on something called yoga to try. Anna's not one of those female humans who bothers much with diet and exercise, says she gets enough of that chasing after me, *BOL*, but she thought this looked like fun and cleared enough space on the floor to get started. I figured I'd keep her company so I bounded over. It took me a while to puzzle out, which I accomplished by poking my nose in various body parts. Anna firmly resisted this fact-finding mission I tried whenever she attempted a new pose, laughing so much she couldn't hold her position.

'Alf" she would say "please do this in your own space, not mine. Okay?"

No, I think not.

She set a long squishy mat on the floor for herself but didn't put one down for me. *What, I don't need one because I am a dog?* Frustrated with my efforts to share, I sat back miffed. It didn't appear to me that Anna had any talent for this yoga thing, but I did.

We dogs had the sense to have been doing this for generations. Did you ever watch your fur pal stand up? Did you notice that every time he did he stretched out his legs, his back and neck and often shook it all out afterwards, and let's not forget one of those positions is titled with us in mind - downward dog.

I, being the expert at this pose, tried to help Anna with all her attempts to achieve the proper position, but let's be honest here, humans are not coordinated, or graceful. Instead of taking her cue from me, trying my best to demonstrate the way the pose should be done, she collapsed in giggles when I landed on her head or when she peeked under her arm and caught me right next to her, staring quizzically from the floor with my butt up in the Aire to be sure she understood. *What the woof*? Oh well, we had a blast. Wonder what she will try next.

One super hot day a friend of the pawrents made a surprise visit with his two Dales. This event got me spinning with excitement, and I didn't stop until we all settled in the outside cage to let the humans talk in comfort. One of the visitors, a foxy female about a year old rated a ten on the cuteness scale. While I was excited to see members of my tribe, one or two runs up and down the garden were more than enough for me but not for this little girl. She had more zip than I've ever seen and did not appear to recognize the word obedience, so while the rest of us relaxed with a drink, she tore around at full Aire-speed, investigating every square inch.

Stretched out near Harry, I couldn't avoid listening as he droned on to his friend. The man said they moved from cooler weather up north somewhere where the pups had been born. The lady in question, cuteness not withstanding, had no idea the problems Florida heat could cause, especially the high humidity, which makes it harder to breathe. We all admired her joy in life, but she ran around like a windup toy with no off button and I started to worry.

With a little nudge from me, by way of pacing in front of the door, the humans discovered her still tearing around and pulled her inside. Took them long enough if you ask me, but they were only humans after all. She stood panting as if her life depended on it and her tongue turned bright red, a sure sign of approaching heat stroke. I think she must have been a few crackers short of a bone as her grin never faltered and she stayed ramped up to the max.

The humans all gave her the once over and agreed she showed no other symptoms. Anna and Harry left their guest and went inside after telling him to only allow her a small drink. Harry reappeared moments later with a large fan he turned up high. It made a lot of noise and did provide a bit of breeze, so may have been of some help but not as much as it would have been for a person, because of course, dogs are different.

Then Anna came back with a wet towel and draped it over Lily, pouring some tepid water over her feet and head. A short while later, to everyone's relief, including mine, the pup perked up, back to her normal self. Woofs to the humans. If they hadn't been watching, Lily might have fared much worse.

Generally speaking dogs can stay outside in temperatures up to ninety degrees for several hours. Of course, I mean with water and shade available, not running around like a manic squirrel. I often like to go out and sit in the heat of the sun for a while myself. Anna is confused by this because on every other occasion I avoid the heat like I do the bathtub.

If only I could tell her, I would. These small sunbathing occasions allow me to absorb some vitamin D and then I lick my fur to absorb the vitamins. Sometimes I like to sprawl on my back too Aireing out my bits, you might say, *hee hee*. Sorry, I am easily distracted, a character trait I could do without. So, as I said, for safety's sake, only allow your fur-kid to be in temperatures over ninety for a maximum of fifteen minutes. Those little guys with flat faces should be out for even less time and be sure to be careful. Hot surfaces like those black tarry road surfaces can result in bad burns on the paws.

While I'm woofling away on this subject, please people, do not shave your fur-kid in the heat thinking it is helping to keep them from overheating. It is not, may in fact be causing sunburn. I think I may have mentioned this before, but just in case I didn't, please take note.

The hot weather got worse and appeared to worry the folks. They sat talking together in soft tones having some kind of intense discussion. Then things got weird and I felt it too. I started feeling anxious and restless because something wasn't quite right with me. Wondering what, I twitched my nose and ears searching for the source like a radar antenna. I flinched a little when the difference in the air caused a sharp prick in my snout as I touched something. My body tingled and I felt uncomfortable. Even my joints hurt.

This is how we pooches figure out something bad is coming. I couldn't explain this in human terms, couldn't understand it even if I could but Anna could. It turns out a change in the air pressure triggers differences in something called an electromagnetic field. The static caused by this is what made me anxious and charged me, like it does you when your hair stands up, for example. Our thick paws and fur coat, prevented it from escaping. My superdale specialized sensory organs (*how was that one eh?*) let me discover it, but did not clue me in, and turning to my family for answers, I found myself unable to get their attention.

They started running around like ants on a march, moving the furniture into piles and bringing things in from the cage room, shouting directions and banging things about. I got a little put out about this, having my comfy snooze so loudly interrupted. *What is wrong with the furniture the way it is?* My mood did not improve as the humans got noisier and more energetic.

They turned the house into an obstacle course and I had to keep moving to avoid being crushed by something. Good grief, I barely had space to move from one room to the next and I couldn't find my bed at all, not that I would be able to use it with all this ruckus going on. I began to think they had both gone crazy, though their antics at least provided a little distraction from my own discomfort.

Done with turning the house upside down, they began carrying things into the cage room from outside and piled them up near the walls. I kept tabs on them, mystified. *What were they up to now?* When I went out to do my business I found Harry busy tying up my Aireboat so it wouldn't move. *Guess we wouldn't be taking a boat ride any time soon.* I inspected every inch of the garden and found nothing except green stuff. *Huh!* My ears picked up the sky bangs and flashes from miles away, too far for humans to hear, and I knew whatever was coming would be here soon.

After these crazy people tired of messing with the garden stuff, things quieted down a little at least for Anna and I. Harry went shopping and came back a while later with several pieces of grass which he laid in the room where the car lived. Naturally I chased after him to inspect the purchase. "That's for you Alf." He said.

For me? Whatever would I want with that tiny patch of grass? I was even more mystified when he put a cup under me as I performed my business. He almost caused me to fall over as I tried to put some polite distance between us, outraged by Harry's invasion of my privacy. Then he poured the contents over the patch of grass.

I walked over and sniffed it to make sure. *Yes, that is my message liquid, no doubt about it.* I could not fathom what Harry intended to do with the spoils of his ill-gotten gains, but not one to stew about such things I just chalked it up to yet more people craziness.

I left Harry stacking bottles of water on the shelves and went to find Anna. She was doing something equally barmy, filling the bathtub with water. Strange time of day to take a bath, but it turned out not to be for her and she didn't try to trick me into one either, so I wasn't worried. Nevertheless I poked my nose over the side and sure enough, it was cold water. *Double huh.* I took a short break to sit down and scratch my ear wondering what would come next. I soon found out when Harry came marching in to the eating table, arms full of those little lamp things and flashlights he likes so much. I don't like those. He moved them around creating shifting shadows which made me jumpy. He did only light them enough to check that they worked, then placed them around the TV room. I hoped I didn't knock them over.

The house now resembled an overcrowded agility course. At last my wacky people declared themselves pleased with their accomplishments and settled down. I did too, dog-tired, *hee hee*, from supervising all this nonsense.

After a nap and dinner Anna snapped on my leash for my nightly business trip. As soon as I poked my nose outside all my senses went on alert and I knew something was coming, in fact, was almost upon us. An impish breeze danced in the bushes and invaded my nostrils with enticing hints of far away scents. I had never encountered a breeze like this before. It blew around like a mischievous live thing but it cooled the weather and I enjoyed my sniff walk, not having to drag along and pant in the heat.

Back in the house Anna told Harry about the wind and they both checked the TV, watching a man talking about the weather. Then Harry went outside and closed most of the shutters making the house feel like a gloomy cave. More madness. Later when I ventured out for my last perimeter check the wind blew much harder, like a live thing, having evil fun at pushing things around. When we got back inside Harry rolled down the shutter in front of the cage room and off we went to bed, but not to sleep.

During the night the wind howled with such ferocious fury it shook the windows. Rain pelted down in torrents and lashed at the house like a raging monster trying to find a way in. Loud bangs, caused by branches hitting the walls and windows shook the doors. We listened to things picked up by the wind go whooshing past. The water surged up, slapping against the walls and carrying with it anything not tied down. Now I understood what all the moving had been about.

The uproar continued, the storm hurling its power against this pitiful barrier, us, so deafening we couldn't sleep. Giving up any attempt at rest, we all got up and went into the sitting room to watch the weather man again. I wasn't scared, you understand, I knew my people would protect me, but I was a bit confused, yes.

One moment we were watching and the next we weren't. Everything went black. Harry got up and I realized why he put lights all over the place. It wasn't so spooky with shadows since he left them all in one place. I'm a dog, so I have no clue what makes the house work, but it left us without light and stopped the whirling things in the ceiling that cooled the air.

At one point Harry carefully opened the front door to scope out what was happening. Peering between his legs I gawked, amazed at an angry sea of water trying to climb up to our front door, rushing up with white caps, as angry as the wind. I worried for a moment I would have to go out into that maelstrom to do my business, but then I remembered that provisions had been made for me. *Whew*. Thank you Great Dog. Harry is strong but he struggled holding that door, forced to use his body weight to slam it shut after a quick gander at the chaos outside.

At the end of a long night listening to the storm trying to blow us away I had to pee. Much to Harry's disgust I refused to use his scrap of grass in the car room. I am an Airedale. I don't use the house as my bathroom. Harry doesn't do that. I did see him pouring some water from the bathtub into the bowl where he pees. He'd never done that before. I gave up trying to decipher the actions of human folk and left him to it. Unlike people, we dogs are able to hold our bathroom needs and that is what I did.

In the morning light all appeared quiet and serene. The house still didn't work and Anna poured the contents of one of those bottles into my water bowl. Because the shutters didn't work, we had to go out the front door. This time Harry came with us. I beelined to the mailbox for a pee, sighing with relief as I donated my Airestream to the already soggy ground. The angry water had disappeared and only after I had taken care of business did I look around.

"No walk for you Alf I'm afraid. A few power lines are down and it's not safe to walk around outside." Harry said. "Let's go check out the back and see how things are there."

Wowzer. The garden had all but disappeared. The fence lay on the ground and parts of it were missing and all the trees were gone; all of them. The boat still sat where Harry had tied it which chuffed him no end. The canal water reached the top of the wall and we stared mesmerized as a neighbor's boat broke free from their dock and ended up lying half under the water before gradually sinking.

The doors were missing from our storage shed but the shed itself still stood, its roof in place but lifted from the walls in some spots. Lots of little square things lay scattered on the ground. I wondered what they were until Harry told Anna, "good thing we have a metal roof. It looks like every one of the neighbors' houses lost roof tiles." My pawrents prevented a lot of damage by stacking everything they could inside the house and cage room.

As we walked back to the front a couple of the neighbors came over to make sure we were all right and I gawped, amazed at all the rubble and tree branches scattered over the road. The neighbors tried to lift the cage shutter for us, straining and shoving, but without the power they couldn't move it. Harry got mad at himself for not having a hand release. "We'll fix that before the next power outage happens." He said. The neighbors did manage to raise the car room door and propped it up letting some welcome air into the house. Good people, our neighbors.

The day remained bright and calm but things didn't go back to normal for many days. We couldn't walk because the roads weren't cleared. My humans couldn't turn on the TV or talk on their phones and the house felt as hot as the box Anna cooked food in. After a confab with the neighbors and looking at everyone's property, Harry said "we've had quite a bit of damage but we are much better off than most."

"Yes" Anna agreed. "We are very lucky. It will take a long time for some of these people to get anywhere near back to normal, if they can at all. It must have been much worse south of us where the storm struck land."

Harry agreed. A little later I heard him talking to a man in the street who told him that a lot of people died, unable or unwilling to get out of the path of the storm. *How terrible.* My doggy brain couldn't wrap itself around the idea that nature could be madder than it had been last night. Harry stayed glum as he cleared branches and palm fronds from our property, placing them in a heap on the other side of the road. We all searched but couldn't find the shed doors anywhere. It took ages to pick up all the roof tiles that had flown all over the place and we propped up enough of the fence that I could go out for my normal routine.

The folks continued to pour bathtub water down their pee bowls and we continued to use Harry's lights at night. I got my dinners as usual but Anna wasn't able to use any of the house things to make their hot meals so they ate sandwiches and other cold stuff. Okay by me. I love sandwiches.

It took a few weeks but when help arrived everyone cheered as the monster trucks drove down the road to fix the overhead wires and the lights came back on in the house. They cleared roads, picking up bundles of branches the size of a car with a gigantic metal claw, and we were able to drive up a ways so Anna could use her phone and check in with all the friends.

She said the shelves were mostly empty in the food store but at least it opened and she did manage to buy some things for us, not an easy job because without power the workers had to add things up in their head, take actual money and figure out the correct change. Life for people is so complicated don't you think? The folks were still eating sandwiches as the box that kept the food cold didn't work during the power outage and everything inside had to be thrown out. When Anna came back from the store she met some neighbors outside and everyone mentioned how thankful they were for what they had as many people's homes had been destroyed. I worried about how the wild critters fared.

Once the power lines were back up I resumed my walks but many weeks went by before the piles at the side of the roads in other areas were taken away and it was safe to travel again. Some of the streets had broken in places and whole neighborhoods flooded. I wondered if my two lady friends were okay.

Nature was awesome. I had no idea such a thing could happen here and I never wanted to experience it again. My humans are so cool. They prepared for the worst and remained relaxed, making sure I felt calm too but they also knew how lucky they had been. They had lived in this part of the country in different places for much longer than I had been alive and been through these storms before, but they both said they had never known one as bad as this one. We stayed close to home for a long time and bit by bit, things began getting back to normal.

SuperDale

POLITICS IS NOT A subject understood by us pooches, but folks have been talking about it a lot of late. I think because Harry just loves to hear himself talk. Anna isn't much into politics so she nods and agrees, knowing Harry wants to provoke an argument - debate, he calls it. Anna doesn't enjoy those. She is a sensible female. Tiring of the latest one, she attempted to distract Harry from his rant about the state of the world. Humans are without doubt the strangest species. Anyway, I found this subject interesting.

"Did you know September 23 is Dogs in Politics Day?"

"What?" Harry spluttered. "Whoever thought that one up? Dogs don't do politics."

I had to agree. True. We have not the slightest knowledge of politics and even less interest in the subject. Probably a blessing we don't.

"Richard Nixon did, if you can believe it." Answered Anna. "According to the story here he denied abusing campaign contributions and in one of his efforts he made a speech during which he talked about Checkers, his Cocker Spaniel. This aroused such sympathy from people that he got to keep his job."

Perhaps thinking this statement would bring on a tirade from Harry, Anna hurried to continue. "Anyhoo, it became a day to acknowledge all the pooches who comfort those in the stressful job of politics. After all, dogs played a huge part in our history and everyone loves the First Dogs."

Too true, I agreed. We probably saved a war or too as well while we were at it.

"A lot of presidents kept dogs." Anna went on, "I expect they were a great comfort, but our sixth president, John Quincy Adams, had another pet, a gator he kept in the east room bathtub."

"I did not know that." Harry said, shaking his head in disbelief. "You have an awesome capacity for unusual trivia." He smiled. "I think maybe a gator makes a much more appropriate pet for politicians, don't you?"

Anna giggled. I wasn't sure whether to agree or be upset so I just tuned them out and curled up for a nap.

The next morning the folks got up before me, an event I could not remember happening before. They got up all smiles and started packing bags. *Yea, road trip.* I got so ramped up I had a barking malfunction and do you know what? The trip was just for me. *Yes.* We're going on a barn hunt. *How do you hunt barns? Doesn't matter, I know hunt alright.* That word had me spinning in circles after so much enforced inactivity

"Alf" Harry laughed, "You'll get dizzy. You're acting like a ferret on speed for goodness sake."

Huh? Okay. I'll go supervise the packing instead. Need to make sure they pack enough treats and my favorite toy. Trotting into the sleep room I spied the bags, packed but still open, and took the opportunity to nose through all of them making sure they included everything I needed. After extensive rooting around I found my stuff at the back in my personal bag. I pulled it all out to give it my nod of approval. Anna had been thorough and hadn't forgotten anything. Satisfied, I went to track Harry down and continue supervising. A while later us guys went out to inspect the wagon almost hitting our heads together as a piercing wail came from the direction of the sleep room. Harry and I looked at each other. *Uh oh.*

"What did you do Alf?" Harry asked with a knowing smirk.

Who me? I met Harry's gaze with puzzled innocence. We both froze, expecting an eruption of some kind but nothing happened except for loud banging noises, as if someone was throwing things at the walls. Harry and I stilled. "What do you suppose that is Alf?"

I pretended to find a new smell to check out, conveying no knowledge of the goings on in the house. Harry *hmm'd* at me, shook his head and went back to work,.

A short while later Anna emerged all smiles. Harry and I were not deceived. She was up to something and we sensed a payback was in the works, what for I could not imagine, but I knew the signs. We remained on alert for a while but all stayed quiet on the Airedale front and although still wary, we relaxed just a tad.

Finished loading the truck, Harry asked Anna with some caution. "All set then are we, ready to start our next adventure?"

"Yep. Let's go." Anna's sweet smile didn't fool me.

Harry got behind the wheel and Anna settled into the seat next to him shutting the door with a bang. *Hey, what about me?* I skidded into the car room a beat behind the others, horrified to find them settled in and all the doors closed.

They wouldn't forget me would they, or punish me for something I didn't know I'd done? My tail went down, my ears drooped low and I dropped to the floor staring up at them with desperate worry, beseeching them with all my being not to leave me behind and alone. An agonizing moment passed before Anna said "hold on for a minute Harry. I think maybe I forgot something" and opened her door. "C'mon then Alf, what are you waiting for?"

Yes. I leapt in, covering her face with joyful licks before settling in my accustomed place.

"That was a bit mean wasn't it?" Harry asked, eyeing Anna with disapproval. "I've seen you hot under the collar before but never mean."

Anna turned and tickled my ears. "It's okay Alf. We never would have left you." Turning back she sighed. "You're right. I meant it to be funny, not hurtful, getting my dander up is no excuse." She gave me another pat. "I should remember Alf is smarter than me and will always win won't you boy?"

I didn't know why she did that but I did feel bad I caused Anna such distress, so there was nothing to forgive. I squeezed between the two front seats and gave them both a grin.

"Okay then" Harry said. "All is right with the world and our little family. Off we go."

Hours later we drove through countryside, so thick with trees the only other thing visible was the road, even from the top of the hills. *Bet I'd find lots of things to hunt in there.* We don't have hills at home so the constant climbing up and dipping down of the car had me running from one side to the other to check out everything. This caught me unprepared when Harry turned sharply because he almost missed the entrance. He drove down a long grassy lane and stopped at a gate barring the way. Climbing out, he discovered it locked and after searching for a latch came up empty, scratching his head as he inspected a gray pad with buttons on it.

"What's wrong?" Anna called.

"I can't get it open." Harry answered turning to Anna with a shrug. "There's no phone here or anything I can see, so we can't get in."

I poked my head out of the window, trying to see what was happening while Anna whipped her phone out and started pushing buttons. After a short conversation she leaned over me to talk to Harry who still searched around for a way to unlock the gate. "Got the code, love. Hop in and we can move on." Harry did and I left my head out of his window anxious to scope out more of this mysterious place.

We hadn't gone too far when Harry drove over an open grassy area and stopped outside a lovely old home built with planks painted white and shutters on the sides of the windows. By now I needed to pee, so climbing out I did just that while I checked out the folks greeting a woman who came out to meet them. After a short talk we all walked over to another building.

It looked like a giant shed, metal with no windows but the entry took up the entire front and stood open like a gaping jaw. This must be the barn I guessed, all but prancing in my hurry to get to the hunt. No go. This hunt, I was told, had rules and Anna and I had to wait until all was explained. The lady droned on and on but at long last Anna and I got to enter.

Bounding in, as much as the leash would let me, I scanned the area on high alert and saw - nothing except rectangles of bound dried grass, but my tail shot up straight and quivered like a tuning fork. I recognized the prey.

Alright, raaatts, let's go. I leapt onto the nearest hay bale, nose to the ground and followed the aroma of rodent, Anna trailing along behind. I don't know how long it takes other dogs but for me this was duck soup. In short order I stopped under a tunnel made of the piled up grass.

Nailed it. I found the rat, a porker-sized one, but now I discovered the rat lady had made the game a bit more difficult because she shut the little pest in a cage. Anna shot up her hand, *Huh, why did you do that?* but she put it down fast as I scrabbled to grab my prey and tugged on my leash hard, jerking me away. I stared at her disapproving glare, dumbfounded but when she waggled her finger at me I surmised with my acute powers of reasoning that actually grabbing the rat was a no no.

The other lady came over to us shooting me disapproving glares and shaking her head. *What sort of game is this?* So disappointing. My people drove all this way just for me to hunt rats and it was all over in minutes. Worse, there was no chasing involved.

I couldn't even sink my teeth into the little creep, who, by the way, appeared totally bored by the whole thing. He was one fat, laid-back rat, must do this every day I guessed. He obviously enjoyed his work and I swear he gave me a smug smirk. My frustration signaled a job well done for him and no doubt, a tasty reward.

I growled, all but gnashing my teeth, and prayed one day his lady would forget to latch the cage allowing one lucky pooch to exact revenge. My people seemed disappointed too but Anna explained to me that this is a competition to find the best rat hunter and had been my first training session. *Pooh. Boring.* Why would any of my tribe want to waste their time doing this when they could never chase or catch the little beasts?

Affronted I stalked outside the barn and sat with my back to everyone while they did their thing. The area intrigued me, surrounded by lush woods with strange plants. *Wait*. My amazing schnoz detected a critter near by, one I didn't recognize, right at the edge of the barn building. I made a beeline for it aggravated to find myself pulled up short by the rat lady.

"Oh no you don't young fella. That's a fox den and she has kittens, so they are off limits, but I'm impressed by that big nose of yours."

Huh, there wasn't going to be any hunting here. Dejected I waited for my folks to get in the car and off we went. I felt sorry for them coming all this way for something they thought would be fun for me. *Woof, I could have more fun in our back garden chasing lizards.*

I perked up later when we stopped in a small town. Harry parked in front of a cafe that sported a lovely garden outside the front entrance. We all settled at one of the tables and someone set it up with all the strange things humans need to be able to attack their meals. *Weird huh?* When he left, a young girl came out and presented me with a bowl of water and *wowzer*, a sausage. *Yes, score.*

I didn't rate sausages often and they topped my list of favorite things. I loved that young girl and grinned up at her, rewarding her with lots of licks and presenting my paw. Things were looking up.

It took less than a nanosecond to polish off a sausage and while still licking my lips, I looked around. A young couple sat at another table with a munchkin. The adults were busy talking and I watched with interest as the wee human took the opportunity to wander off. It became clear right away that she headed, with impressive speed, for the road where the cars whizzed by. I had been taught to avoid these metal things on wheels and realized the danger so I jumped up and barked, pawing at Anna's knee.

"Alf whatever is going on with you. Settle down please."

Not understanding, Anna glanced around and then went back to talking to Harry. The small one had beat feet fast enough to be perilously close to the road. In desperation I tugged hard, succeeding, for once, in releasing the leash from Anna's usually vice-like grip, and raced across the grass. I reached the munchkin just as she put one foot off the curb and seized the back of her dress, tugging hard. We both went down in a heap, safely on the grass. The girl's family at last discovering her gone, stared in horror, too far away to help. They raced over and snatched her up, hugging her tight. The little girl, unaware of the danger, giggled and reached down to grab my hair.

Then chaos broke loose. My people arrived out of breath and grabbed my trailing leash. The little human squealed to be let down. Her family hugged me Airetight, something I'm not fond of but I allowed it. My people hugged me. The other people all hugged me until I couldn't take it anymore and shook myself free. *Didn't people understand dogs don't like hugs?* When more sausages appeared under my nose I stopped worrying.

After a while, everyone calmed down and I tried a nap, my belly full of sausages but I perked up one ear when the small human's people began chatting with my pawrents. It turned out they owned a play place for dogs and they insisted I come to join their regulars while Harry and Anna took a couple of days off to do people stuff in this new town. *Yes, all day play dates*. It couldn't get any better. Dismal rat hunting forgotten I sat up in the back seat of my Airemobile proud and majestic now that I understood I saved a little life. Of course, any other dog would have done the same thing but I felt very king-like all the same and lapped up all the TLC people wanted to give me. For a time. As soon as we made it into our room I scrambled up on the bed, as is my right, scooched it until it met my comfort satisfaction and flopped down with a deep sigh, asleep before my head hit my paws.

The next morning the folks dropped me off at daycare. If you read my last diary you know I have no love for crowded daycares and, in fact, had the honor of being kicked out for conduct unbecoming, but that was then and this is now. I knew enough about these people to trust them if they said I would have an excellent adventure. As we turned onto the private drive an enormous overhead sign proclaimed Dogwood. *Huh?* Wonder what that meant, but as we parked and walked in I found out. Someone decorated the inside of the building with old-style wooden house fronts like the ones on TV of the old west with horses and cowboys and stuff. Outside in the play area I found more western-themed areas like a corral, and the helpers all wore cowboy gear. I was relieved to see no whips or guns, although I couldn't think why there would be. I saw about twenty potential playmates roaming about in a grassy area so big I couldn't make out the fence. Farther out I spied a watering hole for those who hankered for a swim. I loved this place. Perhaps it should have been called Happy Tails because we were all wagging ours and carrying them around like flags.

I kept an eye peeled but no other Airebears arrived. I missed members of my own clan but I greeted all my playmates for the day in our universal language and we wasted no time racing around chasing each other, then resting up in the shade and starting all over again. I'm not sure about others but Airedales, in general, prefer the company of one or two other dogs at a time. Did you know that? *Yes.*

Humans have rules for play and we do too, four of them, for fair play, - ask first, be honest, follow the rules and admit when you are wrong. Due to our super powers we can mind-read with precision, fine tune on the run and keep track.

That's why, if you watch, you will see one dog chasing another and after a bit they will reverse roles. It is almost unknown for any of us to have a disagreement because we know how to behave. I don't think that works with the little human creatures too often. Too bad, not much is better than play.

It felt like no time had passed when my folks arrived to pick me up and carry me back to the big house, exclaiming over the souvenir cowboy hat I wore and which I refused to take off because those lovely people had given it to me. The munchkin's family who owned the place treated me like the royalty I am and I made sure to give them lots of licks to say my proper thank you. How I wished for a place like this in our home town but our county is small without much in the way of businesses. What daycares operated there were smaller, overcrowded and boring. Oh well. Almost too pooped for dinner, almost I said, I did manage a few bites, before stretching out on the bed and crashing. Anna told me later I lay on my back and snored. *Rude.*

Howloween

I ALWAYS LOOK FORWARD to this time of year when the days start to shorten and cool enough to make the days baireable. This year, a new menace arrived with the weather. Every time I went outside the grass irritated my legs and I couldn't resist biting the tops of my paws. It got so annoying I avoided stepping on anything except the hard driveway or road stuff. Then my body started to itch.

I scratched myself all the time and succeeded only in making it worse. This resulted in one spot getting so itchy I bit it raw and it wouldn't heal, I suppose because I wouldn't leave it alone. A hot spot Anna called it. She put one of Harry's tee shirts on me but that made things worse because the aggravation continued and I couldn't reach it now. So, of course, off we went to the dog doc again. He scratched my skin with something and sent me home with some medication.

A few days later we went back for the results of my skin tests. I couldn't believe the news. I am allergic to practically everything, all types of food and many grasses. *Grass!* How could I go outside if the grass caused this awful itching to continue, and worse, the doc ordered my food taken away again, my treats too. I endured three months of mushy food prescribed by the vet last year but it turns out I even had an allergy to the ingredients in that and now had to start again with a different brand of food.

Anna reluctantly fed me this bland, gross-looking stuff that she said the doc charged an arm and a leg for. She still sported all hers so I wondered who she paid him with. She said I had to eat the vet's grub, and only that for three months. I suppose I should be grateful we have less taste buds than people. Can't say that brought me much joy. I was bummed. *How could this have happened and why now, why not earlier, what changed?*

Glum and brooding, I remembered a story Anna recently read me about a dog sentenced to life for killing a Pennsylvania Governor's cat in 1924. I wondered if the unfortunate fella also suffered from allergies and they caused such frustration, that being teased by a cat became the end of the line for him.

One of the joys of life is food and for me, life was looking rather joyless. How could any self-respecting dog survive without treats? Not so much as a crumb passed under my nose. I'm sure you're sick of hearing about the allergy woes over the years, I am too but it looms large in my mind, creating such misery for so long.

Several weeks later the same slop still found its way to my dish at mealtimes. Anna and Harry kept a sharp eye on each other to make sure they weren't tempted to give me something juicy. Of course I encouraged them to do just that by sitting almost on top of them wearing my most mournful expression. I got some satisfaction from knowing they had to fight their willpower and were tortured by my apparent suffering, but alas, scored nothing but my dry, bland food. I did admit the itching went away and my hot spot cleared up though I thought it a high price to pay. We went back to the doc to check my condition and received the awful news that I still needed to stay on this horrible diet. To add insult to injury the doc poked me with a needle to help relieve the itching.

I do believe the man gets a charge out of that. They should keep sharp instruments away from him and give them to someone who derives less pleasure from their use. As if that wasn't enough, my favorite lady assistant came in. About to greet her with some eager licks I almost bit my tongue when she grabbed my butt and poked her finger in, giving me a painful squeeze. *Yikes and whines. What is happening to my life? Is this what getting older is all about?*

Not content with this torture, Anna decided my hair had grown too long and might be adding to my itchy woes. She had the temerity to call me a hairy baire and so the next week in I went for a spa day, one of my favorite things - not.

I liked my groomer lady but being a bit of a mess this time I endured hours of standing still, after the mandatory bath, while she worked on me, followed by the hated nail trim. Being an Airedale and well versed in this ritual, I put up with all of it with practiced stoicism, neither resisting nor making life easy for the workers, who I had to admit, took care to be gentle and talked to me all the time. Nevertheless, I refused to give them even a tiny inkling I approved. They needed to know that I only tolerated all this fuss because I am a gentleman.

When Anna arrived to pick me up I happened to be roaming around near the door. As a favorite of the groomer lady I was entitled to perks and she accorded me these privileges as my due. Anna looked all around at the other dogs, until I almost tripped her up as she wandered into the spa. She looked at me and then said to the greeter girl, "that's a very handsome Airedale you have but someone told me Alf is ready for pick up. Where is he?"

Funny Anna, haha, but as I passed the door I got a glimpse of myself in a mirror and almost did a double take myself. Not having seen my image in quite a while I paused to preen.

The groomer struggled to suppress a giggle but managed and with a straight face, cleared her throat and rolled her eyes in my direction. I had indeed grown into a gorgeous version of myself. Anna walked around me in a circle, twice, clearly amazed. "You are a magician. I have never seen Alf look so handsome. Can I take a picture of you with him so that within the hour when he turns back into the scruffy tramp we're used to I'll have proof he really can look like a proper Airedale?"

Seriously? Methinks Anna spent too much time around Harry today. If she kept it up paybacks could come her way too. Hmph.

My groomer lady knelt next to me for the pic and at the last second when I judged Anna ready, I stuck my tongue out. *That'll show her, so rude.*

Undeterred, Anna waited me out until she got the photo she wanted. I don't know what it is with humans and pictures, but perhaps these spa days might be worth the bother after all, so long as they didn't happen often that is. *Anyone want my pawtograph?*

The days rolled by and I started losing weight as I lost interest in the stodgy mess that served as food. Anna retreated to her computer again. My family were just as unhappy with my diet. They even took to trying to hide their snacks to avoid the guilt of enjoying something I could not share.

Then one blessed day I activated the Airedale signal when a package arrived at the door. I stood blocking the entrance to inspect the item before allowing it passage. Once I gave it my approval, Anna opened it, with my impatient assistance, and lo and behold, it revealed a jumbo bag of dog food, normal looking dog food.

"Yes, Alf. I searched every food on the market and I found just this one that doesn't contain a single item you are allergic to and they sell treats too. I sent for some. Shall we try it?"

Shall we? You betcha. I followed Anna, nose glued to the bag and stood over my dish focused, like a hawk as she poured a small amount in to test. The sniff test said yummy so I got to tasting.

Hmm, different texture, softer than kibble, but it produced a variety of different flavors, all of them yummy. Yes, it's real food. I beamed at Anna, before licking my dish of every speck and she beamed right back at me.

"I'm so glad Alf. The vets mean well but they don't always know other solutions are available, but we do. Don't we?"

Yes we do, thank the big dog in the sky, and you too lovely Anna.

My much improved mood grew to defcon one when Harry told me, another meet with the cousins was coming up soon, *woofs. T*hey called this one Barktoberfest. I cocked my head. *Why?*

"Because it's Halloween, Alf. You remember, that day all the kids dress up and go out and collect candy."

Yips, yeah, it's going to rain candy.

The little ones made easy marks for the good stuff. I spun in circles. *okay, that was almost worth getting my groom on.* At least that's what I thought until Anna butted between us guys.

"They're giving a prize for the best costume this year" she said. What shall we go as?"

"Prize for who?" Harry asked. "Us or the dogs?"

"Both. We could all go as the same thing or in different costumes, any ideas?"

What, I had to dress up again? Sheesh. There's always a price to pay, and I looked so sharp after my spa. Now my gorgeous makeover would be ruined and the humans would make me look ridiculous. The only consolation to this was that all my cousins would be subjected to the same torture.

"We don't have much time to decide" Anna said, "so they will have to be something simple.

How about a ghost? On second thought, maybe not. Someone once told me President Regan's spaniel, Rex, wouldn't enter the Lincoln Bedroom in the White House, which is supposed to be haunted. I forgot that dogs have incredible sensitivity to spirits with those super powers of theirs, don't want to upset them."

Harry and I exchanged relieved looks. Harry didn't like dressing up much either. After a lot of talk and much rooting around in the clothes room, with which I happily assisted, the folks decided to go as hippies.

Hmm, don't know what hippies are, but not going to spend much time wondering either.

That left me. *What is my fate to be?* I waited with trepidation while my pawrents stood staring at me, suggesting one thing then shaking their heads and starting again. Anna dug out one of her dogalogs the mailman brought on a regular basis and began leafing through it but shook her head, not finding anything suitable I suppose.

I wondered if this prize, which so far had been nameless, would be worth it. Seemed like a lot of fuss about nothing to me but I sat on my haunches, resigned to the inevitable.

When the day came I forgot my snit in my joy at seeing my cousins again, no matter what they looked like. I bairely sat still in the car forgetting my distaste for big fast roads and barked my welcome as soon we turned on the street to our field, not waiting until I caught sight or scent of them. I knew we were there. *Yeah.*

Anna struggled to keep me in the car when we parked. "Hold your horses, Alf, though I suppose I should say hold your dogs."

Not funny Anna.

"We have to put your costume on."

Oh oh.

I had to admit both Harry and Anna looked boss in their costumes, long hair, lots of beads, billowy clothes. If I was a betting dale my bones would be on them for winning first prize. As for me, I had not a shred of doubt the prize would be mine. Harry bless him, insisted my costume be something masculine, *thanks Harry*, so I didn't object too much. In fact, though I would rather bite my tongue than admit it, I was delighted with it and gave Anna a paw stomp of approval.

They made me a pirate. Not just any pirate, but Captain Jack Sparrow, *yip*, one of my heroes. I had a pirate hat with a bandana under it to which Anna attached dreadlocks strung with beads, and a wide leather strap draped over my shoulder. Along with that I wore a pirate's jacket and the back bore the printed words 'trick arr treat.' Last but not least, the item every self-respecting pirate needs, an eye patch. Once dressed, my people nodded at each other and smacked hands.

"Perfect." Harry said as he adjusted my hat. "He looks every inch the ruffian that he is and that patch makes him a real brigand. After all, he has more than a bit of a pirate in him. If I didn't know better, I'd swear he just smirked at us."

Well, I did. I still had some facial expressions left in my repertoire that I hadn't displayed. If humans think they have seen my whole bag of tricks they are mistaken. My crew had outdone themselves and I not only didn't object I strutted out with pride, by far the best competitor in the group. Naturally I won the prize. How could it be otherwise? And my people took a zillion pictures, clicking away with their little phone boxes.

After the prizes were awarded and costumes discarded we pups raced off to the far corners for some doggy catchup. A woofing great day, yes, only marred by the fact I couldn't score any food, even with my best efforts. Everyone had been told not to feed me. *Abuse, yes?* People and dogs alike scarfed up goodies wherever I looked. but despite my finest stalking procedure I scored not a crumb. Nothing for little me, a pitiful state of affairs. *When would this torture end?*

As if that wasn't enough, a few days later, while trying to get comfy for a nap, I discovered it hurt when I sat down. *Good grief, what now?* At first I ignored it, hoping it would go away, but no such luck. By the evening I stopped sitting down altogether. Humans can be pretty slow on the uptake but Anna eventually noticed something amiss when she spotted me pacing around in a curved position.

"Alf, whatever is the matter? Come over here and tell me about it."

I did as she asked but instead of checking out my impressive rear end, she proceeded to clean my ears. *What the fluff woman!* I shook my head in protest. When would people learn to talk Dale, or at the very least learn to interpret the detailed and obvious signs we gave them? *Sigh.* No clue. Just as I began to despair Harry walked in. He took one look and said "Anna, what's wrong with Alf's butt?"

Anna stopped peering in my ears and instead turned me around, squeezing and poking all over my butt. She had to do this because of my thick hair, still dense despite the groom. After she'd taken liberties for some time from my long-suffering self she exclaimed "found it."

"Found what?" Harry asked.

"There's a staple in his butt."

"Get out." Harry exclaimed. "Alf, how on earth did you manage to staple your butt?"

I had no clue what a staple was, let alone how I did it. I peered at my butt in trepidation. I could feel something hard and irritating in my behind biting me. Thank Dog it wasn't a vicious bug of some kind.

"Okay" Anna said. "We can fix this."

This would hurt. I knew it, and it did, though to give Anna her due she tried to be gentle. The thing somehow lodged itself in a delicate place between my legs and just underneath the curve of my rear end. I tried hard not to squirm or jump away but intense pain is difficult to ignore you understand. I am an Airedale and do not allow any discomfort the satisfaction of a response but today, sad to say, my stoicism got up and left. However, I did not whine or cry, didn't even yip. A minute later Anna held up the offending item in triumph.

"No idea how you did this Alf. If it was on the floor somewhere I can't figure out how it stuck you, but it did. You have a little wound here, so hang on while I shave some hair and then put something on the area to help it heal."

Oh, the embarrassment. Would the torture never end? Anna was quick with the clippers and whatever she put on the cut soothed my wounded butt. To my immense relief the torment stopped and I could sit without discomfort. *Whew.* I curled up in my bed to recover. I couldn't even look forward to dinner.

Aire travel

THIS IS ONE OF MY favorite times of year. The weather has cooled and I get to visit my cousins again and this trip coincided with a gorgeous day. We met in the meadow owned by one of our human friends, which by itself is worthy of a joyous run. I knew where we were going so as our car approached the gate I pushed forward to see better, my head pressed up against Harry, and let loose ecstatic woofs in his ear making him jump. Lucky for me he had already stopped the car to open the gate. As we drove in, some of my friends surrounded us yapping greetings. Anna had to climb over them to release me from the car. Wriggling with impatience I leapt down and we all raced off to the far corners for a private doggy reunion.

When we emerged a while later more pals had arrived, about thirty all told and we wore ourselves out catching up with new friends and old. After a while we ran out of steam and rested in the shade of a tall oak. Not for long though.

Various calls and whistles rounded us all up and surprise, the humans had built a fort in the middle of the field. Squinting, I recognized the arrangement, hay bales.

Not another barn hunt. Again. Ho hum. Perhaps this time would be different but it wasn't.

I sat apart with my people as the others lined up to try their first hunt. They all had the same reaction, starting with intense excitement and ending up frustrated and disappointed.

When it came to my turn, instead of nosing around I sauntered in a straight line and stood next to the rat in the cage, not deigning to dignify its existence with even a scornful look. The lady in charge of the lesson shook her head at me but I didn't care. I just wanted to join my pals who were creating a hullaballoo at the far end.

Racing over to join the fray, I put my schnoz to the ground and was hit with a tantalizing scent before I'd even taken a sniff. *Activate tails guys.*

I vaguely heard someone calling but didn't pay any mind to unimportant outside stimuli. My nose turned on and my ears turned off in the approved Airedale hunting manner. The pack followed me, showing impressive restraint in not baying like a pack of hounds. I tracked around bushes, crawled under an old vehicle, jumped rocks and spied a deep hole hidden by weeds. *Just call me Indiana Bones.* I dived on in, crawling through the tunnel and out another exit. *Darn it, the prey left us in the dust. Oh well.*

Anna finally managed to get my attention, scolding me for disappearing. "Get a dog they said. It'll be fun, they said." She muttered, giving me a glare that would have shriveled the bravest soul. "Alf, look at yourself, covered in half the bushes around here. Did you forget that we are having our pictures taken today?"

Wait, what? Yes, I did.

Every year at this gathering we all took turns posing for pictures with our humans. Harry and Anna mailed ours to their friends about the same time they started putting up decorations in the house and bringing in a tree. So now I had to submit to a sprucing up and to having my face and beard combed. Anna managed to make me look respectable enough and I got quite enthused, preening as I sat on the table while the servants fiddled with the camera thing, that is until Anna dumped a ribbon of bells round my neck and a really dumb looking hat on my head. Affronted, I glared at the camera thing with my best stink-eye, after I refused to look at it at all that is. After a while I got bored but knew I couldn't go play with my pals until I cooperated so I sat and posed with them until everyone proclaimed themselves happy, then back to the gang.

Aware that pictures meant we were at the last meet of the year, I did not expect to go on any more trips for a while but a few days later Harry took a call and then told Anna he had to go away for a meeting on the other coast. A long debate followed this pronouncement to which I paid close attention, ears twitching at warp speed for better reception.

Yes, I had it right.

We were going to travel again. This time we were going all the way across the state. By now I had morphed into an expert traveler so I kept my cool and did my self-appointed duty supervising the pawrents as they rushed around packing and doing this and that. Then off we went. This trip took us on rural roads and I kept amused, much to Anna's annoyance, talking to all the cows and horses we passed along the way. I didn't see cows often, so I was excited to greet them all.

The fields were full of them along with lots of strong, enticing smells. Traffic forced Harry to drive slowly allowing me to eyeball everything we passed. He fixed that later by turning onto one of those super fast roads he much prefers, I can't think why, and there we stayed until our destination came into view.

Wow, this new boarding house sat right on the edge of the endless water (ocean to you). My kind were not allowed on the beach, but I could view the goings on from the balcony. I inspected the room and gave it my sniff of approval despite the unacceptable noise level raised by people coming and going outside all the time.

After dinner I positioned myself at the door and woofed, growled and roared when footsteps came too near. Had to protect my people from unknown strangers, didn't I? To my astonished disbelief, my sentry services were not appreciated and I was ordered away from my post. I tried my best to earn my keep and the lack of appreciation saddened me, but as we all know, humans are an ungrateful lot. Settling down to sleep I wondered what the next day would bring.

Well, as it happened it was disappointing. We drove to a pretty area with lots of houses. Harry met a guy in one of them and it turned out this person didn't like dogs. *Can you believe that?* A defective trait in my opinion, and therefore not a person I thought Harry should be going to meet, but no one listened to me.

Anna and I were banished to wait outside. A lady brought a chair for Anna to put in the shade but the biting bugs attacked with astonishing ferocity and we ended up taking a ramble around the block a few times to escape them. Harry's meeting seemed to go on forever but at last he emerged and back we went to the hotel.

I loved going on trips but this one turned out to be a bit of a bummer. Maybe I had gotten so used to them that they became ho hum. *Not.* We relaxed in our room for the rest of the day and I looked forward to the next morning. The folks gazed at the TV for a while and became animated when the weather man started talking a lot but I ignored the noise, already snoozing in my house which I now agreed to use, deeming enough time had passed to make it an acceptable abode.

The morning started with a phone call from downstairs which resulted in the folks spending so much time on their phones they quite forgot me and the need for my morning ablutions. I had my legs crossed by the time Anna remembered. She rushed me downstairs, onto the grass and back upstairs again.

This did nothing to improve my mood and I became quite concerned about the tense vibes coming off my people in Airewaves. Anna rushed around packing our things.

Were we leaving already? Why the rush?

Harry's mood grew distracted as he grabbed his keys and left for a while, returning some time later looking distraught. "Are you ready?" He asked Anna without pausing for an answer.

"Yes. We've got everything. Did you manage to get some gas."

Harry nodded. "Yes. I was lucky, going out earlier than most. I've checked us out too. We need to hit the road now."

I still had no idea what was going on but I found out when a female outside the room asked Anna a question as we passed by.

"Yes, Anna said. "There's a strong hurricane expected to make landfall here later this evening. They're evacuating the hotel."

Woofles. That explained why I felt out of sorts this morning. Another one of those scary storms coming? This was becoming more than tiresome.

"But", said the lady, "we're here on a cruise, only ashore for today. What are we to do?" The poor woman looked quite befuddled and so scared she was close to tears.

"Oh my." Anna shook her head. "I'm so sorry. I'm sure the cruise line would have sent someone to help. They're probably downstairs to organize things. They wouldn't just leave you." She patted the woman on her arm and said with a smile, "you'll have quite the story to tell everyone from this vacation."

The lady didn't smile but thanked her and hurried away. Now I understood. We'd already been through one of these storms a while ago but this time we were being turfed out without shelter. No wonder my people were distraught. I kept next to Anna as we made our way down to the entranceway which looked like a madhouse. People scurried all over the place, the noise of their voices at a pitch distressing for me. I'm an Airedale you understand so I wasn't frightened and tried my best to send calming signals to the other pooches running around with their people and feeding off their emotions.

When we walked outside we found Harry had packed all our stuff in the car. He stood guard, waiting for us. He shook his head at all the people milling around with no apparent purpose.

"This is just dreadful. These people have probably never been through anything like this before. I heard accents from a dozen different countries. I hope someone has arranged shelter for them somewhere." Climbing into the car with me, Anna agreed.

Well, I have to tell you, that was a trip like no other. We needed to go south according to Harry, but first we had to travel north on the super-fast road, only today it wasn't even close to fast. The road wasn't crowded but it looked like nothing was moving. It didn't take long before we started weaving around parked vehicles with no-one inside. Some people had even left the doors open. It looked like one of those disaster movies Harry liked to watch.

Anna looked around in amazement. "What's happening Harry?"

"They ran out of gas. Cars lined up around the block at every station by the time I got ours. They're probably all closed now with no more gas for sale. Folks got on the road anyway and had to abandon their vehicles when the tanks were empty. Before long there likely won't be any power either, or cell phone signals. There are a lot of people in this area. It's a port town and popular. It will be a madhouse here. Here we are, at last." Harry made a few turns and before long we found ourselves back on the same road headed in the opposite direction. Only this time, I stared in amazement at a completely empty road.

"Nice." Harry said, smiling at last. "They must be getting ready to close the road in this direction. We'll make good time and try to reach our exit before it's reopened to go back the other way. That's what they do when these storms occur, open the roads to go in one direction so more people can leave town more easily."

I sat in the back seat, taking everything in. I know when it's important to remain shush, so that's what I did, not the least because we were flying. No other cars meant no police patrols and Harry took full advantage, speed freak that he is. Despite the lack of other cars, the pouring rain slowed us down and it took several hours before the folks relaxed and we left the fast road behind. The storm had already passed this area, leaving in its wake an eerie quiet and a carpet of broken trees. The folks' relief didn't last long. Attempting to turn in the direction he wanted, Harry stopped in a hurry because barricades stretched across the road denying access and a police officer waved him away.

Anna buzzed her window down. "What's going on here deputy?" She asked.

"Road's flooded" he responded. "You can't go this way. Turn right here."

With no other option we turned right. It so happened at that point in our trip we were in the middle of nowhere with no idea where to go and Anna wasn't able to use her phone for directions. Harry started muttering under his breath and we drove quite a ways like that before the muttering became an explosion. "We've no idea where we are or where we're going and if we keep on going this way we'll run out of gas."

Harry's temperament, much more volatile than Anna's began to build steam. These kind of human emotions transfer to us, causing stress for us too, and I fixed my stare on Anna, trying to communicate the depth of my anxiety. I panted, waiting for her to diffuse the tension as she usually did and right on cue, she did.

"No worries" said Anna in that soothing tone she used at times like this. "We can't get lost in Florida. If we go east or west at some point we'll reach the ocean. We're headed west, in the right direction and sooner or later we should be able to turn south. We just need to find a good road. I've been watching the traffic ahead of us and it's all making a left turn up there" she said, pointing. "Let's go that way."

Harry shrugged and not seeming to have a better idea, did as she said. Behind them I stayed quiet, wide-eyed with ears alert. This adventure had taken a serious turn. The storm had blasted through this entire area ahead of us and left it's wreckage behind.

Massive trees lay sprawled on the ground, vegetation strewn everywhere. There were no houses, so aside from vast stretches of muddy-looking water where none should be, there was not much other debris.

We had been driving south for some miles now and seemed to be heading for home. We made it without problems for another couple of hours and with relief, recognized the area. Anticipating a smooth trip home, Harry was brought up short by another police officer.

"Sorry sir, can't go this way. The power lines are down, live wires everywhere."

This time the officer gave us directions, but did so quite fast and they were quite complicated. As he was speaking, another driver raced up in a panic causing the deputy to wave us on without any chance to ask for a repeat as he was already turning to the line of people waiting behind us.

I wasn't concerned. Anna is an exceptional navigator. She did make a couple of mistakes, causing us to backtrack, but did direct us, at last to a familiar road not far from home. *Well done Anna. We survived mother nature and conquered the roads, terriers all.*

Back at home, we collapsed in separate heaps, thankful the hair-raising adventure was over. I hoped Harry's meeting had been worth it.

A week or so later I felt a bit low. It seemed some small thing was always wrong with me. While I didn't complain, it was disheartening to never feel at my peak performance. I did finally ditch the itches for the most part, after tons of baths, but the allergies caused some wicked ear problems and so back to the vet we went. I expected the exam and resultant medicine, but not the rest of the treatment. Doc seemed worried about something and talked a while to Anna. I tuned them out until I caught the dreaded word "tests" again. Next thing I knew I found myself in the back room having pictures taken of my insides and then someone put a kind of wrap around my tail and pumped up to squeeze it, *talk about weird*, but at least it wasn't painful.

After all this nonsense Anna and I were left waiting a long time for the doc. We both fidgeted in the cramped little room, exasperated with the long wait until at last the main man reappeared. He put the picture of my insides on the blue screen attached to the wall for Anna to look at.

I couldn't make any sense of it, but Anna's demeanor became grave and that alarmed me. I tried to make out what they were saying but all I caught were the words 'heart is enlarged, grade 3 murmur, and medication'. Now I had drops for my ears and pills for my heart. I trudged back to the car and walked into the house with a droopy head and tail. *Why did I get sick all the time?* I know all this stuff is supposed to fix me but none of my pals had all this trouble and Anna's mood had become troubled. She went straight to her computer and spent the rest of the day on it while I lay with my head on my paws wondering what was going on.

Later Harry came in and I forgot my troubles. He brought me some new treats, allowable with my diet, and we roughhoused for a while. Us guys knew how to play better than the girls. We got so rowdy Anna gave up on her work, closed her screen machine and joined in, back in her familiar chipper mood. Life is grand when my humans romp around with me.

I didn't like the pills, but I did feel better. Anna started adding some liquid to my meals, herbs she called them, not something I would choose as a topper, but not awful, so okay. Then every morning she alternated between putting a hot cloth and a cold cloth on my chest every few breaths or so. Weird but not bad, in fact I quite enjoyed it. She said it would help me and it did. Any time I got pets from my people I felt better.

Thankswoofing Outing

I cheered up more on turkey day. We were all especially thankful this year, causing Anna to spend ages making the scrumptious dinner she cooked up every year. She promised we could risk going off the diet this once and made up a plate for me of turkey and all the trimmings. I was beyond ecstatic at the tantalizing aromas and so enamored I didn't gobble but took my time savoring all the stuff I hadn't enjoyed in ages. My belly full, I retired to my boudoir, and slept that night in true Airedale style, flat on my back, all my paws in the air, dreaming while the taste of my thanksgiving dinner filled my mouth, each and every ingredient.

It had been a while now since that awful trip and we had not ventured out anywhere. We were all content to stay home, but since returning to routine with the speed of a slug, I was ready for something a little more interesting again.

One day Harry announced we would all go to a car show. Harry is crazy about cars. Anna not so much, but an outing is an outing yeah? Did you know there was once an Airedale Car? Yes, a business called Nanson, Barker & Company, in Yorkshire, England, made it. I don't know if any are still around because it was made from 1919 to 1924. Can't think why such a vehicle didn't become world renowned. Too bad I can't tell Harry about it. He would be excited and try to track one down. Wouldn't that be a blast?

During this period of relaxing at home us two guys spent a lot of time watching TV. We mostly watched cars, one of Harry's favorite subjects, dull and uninteresting to me, but I perked up when I spied an Airedale, a handsome looking fellow sitting next to an older gentleman with the requisite car in the background. I pricked up my antennae and paid close attention.

Turns out the owner of this fine looking dude was an inventive human by the name of Ferry Porsche, responsible for the Volkswagen Beetle as well as his namesake car and several others and oh yes, the birth of the tiger tank. Impressive, yes, Harry positively drooled over all these machines, but it turned out this was not a nice man. Not only was he a close friend of that monster Adolph Hitler, a human even I knew about, but he was a member of the SS, those guys who wore the black shirts in WWII, and he used slave labor to make his machines. I suppose all this was forgiven later in his life. I don't know and cared less, but I was concerned that such a human owned an Airedale and could only hope the pooch was treated well and enjoyed a good life. Harry didn't know. Sometimes my brain got boggled by the horrors humans could commit and I preferred not to think about it, only be grateful and thankful for my own good fortune in having such a kind and loving family.

I digress, again. We jumped in the car and rode down to the historic district. The barking lot was full to overflowing and Harry drove around and around looking for a place to park. We both got a bit grumpy until at last Harry spotted a car leaving and we slid into the vacant space. I jumped out and led the way. You don't walk an

Airedale you understand. We walk you, so I trotted down the road, head high, leading my humans until we came to the main street where Harry brought me to a screeching halt. Wheeled machines of every shape and color and age lined the street. *Oh oh.* This was going to take a long time to get Harry down the length of this street and it did.

Anna was about as impressed as I and after stopping at every car while Harry inspected it and talked with the owner, we took off on our own, Anna in search of coffee, me in search of treats. We found both and sat down at a table outside a little cafe, relieved to be able to take a breather from the stop and wait routine.

Everyone made a big fuss of me and I scored a ton of offerings while Anna wasn't watching. I felt a bit guilty, knowing I wasn't supposed to eat anything except my crappy food, but not for long. I scarfed the nibbles down fast before eagle-eyed Anna caught me, and then, best of all, my antenna located one of my tribe sitting quietly with two humans beside an older car a bit further down the street. I nudged Anna's arm almost causing her to spill her drink.

"Alf, why did you do that?" She asked before looking in the direction I pointed. "Oh" she said "I see. Okay, lets go say hello shall we?"

No need to ask me twice. I pranced along like a horse biting at the bit and was rewarded when my target sat up and spied me. His excitement roused his people who stood up to greet us and we both, us dogs that is, spun in circles, so happy to meet another tribe member.

Turns out his name is Clarence. I thought this a terrible name for such a dignified breed as ours but too much of a gentleman to remark on it, I zipped my lips. Our humans spent some time getting acquainted and after the first excitement we settled down companionably as well.

Clarence, we discovered, lived too far away for us to visit, which is a bummer but Anna made sure she put their contact information in her phone in case they ever visited again. We stayed together until Harry finally arrived and then, of course, had to inspect this car.

At last, the car show broke up and we left for the ride home so, in the end we all had a great time. Clarence and I said our goodbyes along with a doggy "live long and pawsper" salute and

I crashed on the sofa, full of treats and doggy dreams, *ahhh*.

Merry Woofmas

THIS TIME OF YEAR brought more of my favorite weather, cool and windy. I love a brisk breeze. It brings loads of new scents with it and when I go outside I sit with my nose in the air and my mouth open, tasting them while I separate them into known vs unknown.

A lot of wild creatures live around us, so this can take some time. Sometimes I envy them being able to roam free but I've seen enough of them out there to know how hard a wild life can be and I do love my family and my comfy sofa so that jealousy is short lived.

Now and again I catch a whiff of a coyote or come across their poop on one of my walks. Once Anna and I saw one on the next street block and we joined in a stare-down until he thought better of an encounter and slunk away. I know them to be opportunistic predators, who hunt in packs. Often they will send out a lone scout to lure an unwary dog into play away from it's home. On occasion they mate with one of us. Did you know a coyote crossed with a dog is called a coy dog? *Yes.* They are part of our family Canis, after all.

Today we met another one. This guy was a lot bigger than me.That's because the eastern coyotes are part wolf, the two species having mated at some time in the past. They are usually most active at night and they are the best at keeping pests controlled, like rabbits for example. They are also super fast, like up to greyhound speed.

I set myself ready to defend Anna, but she's pretty smart for a human and knew to stand her ground with me. She kept eye contact and pulled out her phone which meant she was about to let loose one of those awful loud noises like that air horn thing, but before she could press the button, the coyote turned and tiptoed away. Guess he thought we were too much for him to take on alone. *Hee hee.*

Have you ever seen one on the move? They walk and run on their toes to keep the noise down, cunning those guys. With the coast clear, we also turned, but not tiptoeing, *hee hee*, taking another direction so as to avoid a confrontation.

Back home I headed for my bed, ready to relax after our little adventure but I quickly lost any hope of a snooze. This is the time of year when people get weird. They start stringing glittery things all over the house and exchange the stuff that sits on the furniture surfaces for things that look more like a woodland. I like it. Then they bring in that fake tree that's not worth peeing on and string all kinds of balls and things on it while I nose in the boxes to pick out the best ones. Harry gets out his train set. I do like that and will lie, snout to rail, watching it go round and round but then Anna always butts in after a time to tell Harry he has chores to do. He sits at the table for hours muttering to himself while he writes on little square pieces of paper and puts in copies of those ridiculous pictures we had taken at the meet. I told you it was weird.

The best things though are the smells coming from the kitchen where Anna is so busy she can't deal with me getting underfoot while I clean up for her. It's a thankless task I can tell you. Last, but not least she and Harry smuggle stuff into the house and avoid each other while they wrap up things in boxes and colorful paper. I try to clean up here too but end up with bits of paper all over the house.

Once I got tangled in a string of lights which set Anna laughing so hard she almost dropped her phone trying to film my frantic attempts at escape. *Humph.*

I don't mess with the packages once they are placed near the tree because I can tell which ones are for me. Knowing where they are I'll wait till the proper time to tear off all the wrapping. I help the folks with that too so they can unwrap their presents faster. They are slower than dripping water at paper-tearing. People in general are so much clumsier and slower than us dogs with our superpowers.

The day before Christmas is called Christmas Eve and my family invited several folk to stop by. They were busy all day getting ready, forcing me to trot back and forth between them at regular intervals supervising. They piled so much food on the eating table I couldn't decide which was what but at the appointed time I stayed at my post hoping to be given a sample of each and every one and I'm happy to report I did just that and then some by the end of the evening.

Harry stationed himself at the table for drinks and was mixing various liquids when one of the guests wandered over and asked him what he was doing. Harry said, "I found a recipe in an old book for a drink called The Airedale and in Alf's honor I thought I'd give it a try. Here, have a sip."

The guest did and smacked his lips, "That's good, can I have the recipe?"

"Sure" Harry responded. "Bourbon, Aperol, Simple syrup, Grapefruit zest."

"Aperol you said? I don't think I've heard of that before, what is it?"

It's an Italian liqueur made from rhubarb so they say. I'm not sure what that has to do with Airedales, but oh well."

The guest laughed. "I can see why its called that. It has quite the bite."

Hmm, who is that fella again? I listened to this exchange with interest. *A drink in my honor. Cool, and they liked it. Why didn't they give me one? I* nudged Harry's elbow.

Hey, I'm down here, where's mine.

Harry shook his head. "Sorry Alf. It might be named after your tribe but it's not for dogs. Water is the drink for you pal. Besides, you wouldn't like it. Here, have a sniff." He put his drink bowl under my nose. One whiff and I turned my head. Yep, he was right, *ugh*. People like the strangest things, don't they?

On Christmas morning, like one of the little people, I was up early, running around, trying to get the folks to hurry up and get to the pressies, not that I had any luck. They made me wait while they lingered over breakfast and for once I was more absorbed in the fake tree than in food.

Out of patience I fluffed off to sit under it, head on my paws and, yes, pouting. When I grew weary of that I walked over and laid my head in Harry's lap with a paw on his knee. That did the job, *yea*.

We piled all the goodies in the middle of the room and sat around while Harry looked at each one and then handed one to Anna. By this time my tail drooped with all the thumping it was doing and I danced around nipping at the gift Anna held to help her open it as fast as I could. No go. Anna took her time trying to not damage the wrapping. *Huh, who does that?* We Airedales are not Aireheads and I knew they were teasing me. How slow must people be not to know it is never a good idea to tease a dog? Okay, that's it. Refusing to wait another minute I stalked over to the pile and chose my package.

"Yea Alf, you found one, good job fella." Harry patted my rump as I trotted by just out of grabbing range and lay down to start the lovely fun of tearing it up to find the prize.

My folks stopped opening their gifts to watch me and I kept an eye on them as I worked. I would permit no more delay in opening my stuff. I relaxed as it became obvious they weren't going to interfere. Have you ever argued with an Airedale, hmm?

It didn't take long to shred the wrapping and you'll never guess what I found - a purple snake, yes, and get this, treats hidden inside at various places. Shaking off the shreds of paper, I picked it up and trotted off to the fireplace where I began extracting all the treats inside. *Awesome thing this snake, thank you Harry and Anna, all is forgiven.*

This thing called Christmas is my favorite time of year, all fun and happiness, yes.

Later that week Anna talked on her little box to one of the neighbor people, and being bored, I eavesdropped. These neighbors only moved in a short while ago and were still working on settling in. I saw them once or twice on our walk. They are lovely folk and accorded me my proper due, but if I was hearing right, and I was, I had my ears pricked and fine tuned, they just adopted a puppy. Yea, another dog in the neighborhood. We would be friends and have play dates, *woofs*.

Anna put down her phone and grabbed my leash. "C'mon Alf, let's go meet a new neighbor."

She didn't have to ask me twice, I grabbed my harness from the basket and we were out the door before I could shake my tail.

The new puppy turned out to be a boxer, so tiny that she fit into the neighbor's hands. *Whoa*, boxers are big dogs, bigger than me when grown. This tiny little runt couldn't be a boxer could she? I was not allowed to approach for more than one quick look because she was quite frail.

I listened to Anna ask about this. It turned out the entire litter died. This minuscule female was the only survivor and way too young to be away from her mom. I felt bad for her, even though I was glum that it would be a long time before she grew enough to come play, but she was a feisty little thing, struggling to meet everyone with bright eyes and a happy grin. Pretty she was, I was quite taken. It reminded me of a story Anna read to Harry a few days ago.

Two puppies had been found buried in the ice in the far north of a place called Russia. They were from the same litter and about three months old (plus over twelve thousand years, which was the time the brainiac people said the litter had been born). Anna showed me a picture and they did look a lot like me, brown fur, paws to grow into, big black nose and teeth like mine. Hunters looking for mammoth tusks found them. Anna showed me one of those too.

The find stoked up the brainy people because although we dogs diverged from wolves about 35,000 years ago, they were having a hard time figuring out when we befriended people and these pups were found near a camp where a fire had been used. It is sad these little guys did not live long and likely suffered a miserable death. I hoped my new little friend would do better than that and thrive. Anna said we would visit again when the pup got stronger and put on some weight. I'm glad she lucked into a great family and at Christmas time too.

Anna and I must have been thinking the same thing, that there were many others who weren't so lucky, so the following week we embarked on a clear-out of my stuff. We packed up some of my toys to make room in my toy bin, *huffs, I wonder why,* and a bed I didn't use any more because Harry bought me a different type and I much preferred that one. We also went to the shop and bought a couple of new toys, some dog treats and a hefty bag of food and then off we went to the local shelter.

To be honest, my favorite toys are cardboard and paper. Anna fills a box with crumpled paper and treats and I have the best time tearing it all up to get at the goodies, *yowzer*. I thought the shelter guys would love that too, but probably didn't get the chance, too bad. I was happy Anna included my least favorite toy, a flickstick. I considered this invention beneath my attention. You know, a glorified rope on a pole with a ribbon on the end to chase. Privately I believed some clever salesperson made a bigger one that they made for cats and then renamed it as a dog toy. Not fooling me, whoever you are. I wouldn't touch a cat toy with a ten foot pole BOL.

I was not happy to be in that place. The sadness coming out in waves upset me before even seeing the inhabitants. I wasn't allowed to visit them but the workers who cared for them were all happy and friendly so I knew they were doing their best to find homes for the inmates. They were delighted with all our pressies and said the dogs would be too. They would send pictures of the Christmas party to us. They asked Anna if she would like to go inside but she said no, which is why I couldn't go in either. I understood why she said no. If Anna went inside we would be going home with all of them and Harry would have a stroke.

I felt heartsick they had not found families, but happy we brightened their lives a bit and thankful for my own life. The experience kept me subdued for a day two, wishing every pup could have a good home and a happy life. The shelter workers sent Anna pictures of the party they held for their pack and Anna put her phone down at my level so I could see too.

The humans placed all the toys in an empty room and one by one they let the dogs in to race around and pick out the toy of their choice. I went all soft and gooey seeing how much fun these bros had and that we made their day a little brighter.

Aire dysfunction

WOOFMAS CAME AND went and that terrible night when the sky lit up with terrifying noises. I didn't get too bothered this time because my humans put the TV on at its loudest and closed all the blinds to keep out the flashing lights. They also fed me lots of special treats. I didn't refuse any of them. I would never refuse food but I had been feeling a little stuffed over the holidays and Harry dared to remark I was starting to look more like a porker than an Airedale. *Rude but true.*

The house guests during the holidays proved to be suckers for my starving dog routine. I scored every time I batted my big brown eyes at them, which I did every time my hawk-eyed family looked away but this morning I definitely felt uncomfortable. As soon as the door opened I started eating grass in an attempt to alleviate the ache in my belly. As you know, when we have visitors Anna dresses me up in my best bow tie and it always makes me feel a little educated as well as debonaire, so keep reading, I'm about to deliver some more doggy knowledge.

It's hard to believe, I know, but one breed of canine is almost as interesting as us fellas, the Norwegian Lundehund. This guy has some awesome powers not bestowed on us, like extra toes, moveable ears he can close, flexible shoulder joints that let him lean all the way backwards and a foxlike tail just to name a few. *Pretty rad huh?*

Unfortunately, the reason I bring this up is because he is also prone to a digestive disorder, so much so the medical guys gave it a special name, Lundehund gastroenteropathy, Do you think they could have found a longer word? I never understood why docs for people or pets, couldn't call things by simple names. It boggled my brain trying to figure out why they kept using such odd words so I stopped trying. To continue, this condition can be managed, but not cured. Airedales, I'm pleased to report, do not suffer from this particular condition. As I'm sure you know, we are the proud possessors of one of the most advanced digestive systems. Of course, you do. It's a regular powerhouse. Well, it needs to be.

Our jaws are made in such a way we can only chew up and down. Did you know that? The aim is to pass the food into our stomach as fast as possible. The acid in our stomachs is over one hundred times stronger than yours. If you were to touch it, you would likely burn your fingers, *hee hee* and we have a lot of it, so strong it softens bone matter. Impressive, huh.

We have the quickest processing cycle of any mammals, which means we break down food really fast because our intestines are shorter, and move food through three times faster. We can store food in our stomachs too, for as long as twelve hours, which is why we can last a long time between meals. Don't you wish you could do that?

We don't suffer from colon cancer either. We don't require much fiber in our diet unless we suffer from poop problems or need to manage our weight. *Uh oh. Now I've done it. Anna will be getting out the fiber.* So you can see that the wrong food can mess with our digestive system and then it can't work as it should.

The amount of sausage I'd eaten over the last few days, along with everything else, might well account for my present discomfort. Like people we can suffer from heartburn and, *oops, what was that?* Just then a loud pop and an eye-opening stench jetted from the area of my rear. I jumped up in shock and stared at my tail. *What was that? What is happening? Am I dying? I'd better go outside and chew some more grass.*

Just my luck I had been sitting next to Anna and Harry. They both stared at me as if I had two heads, then wafted their hands in front of their faces.

"Alf" Harry said, "Was that you? Would you mind going outside if you are going to do that please?"

I slunk to the door, checking behind me for more surprises, happy to feel the grass under my toes. I like grass, it's sweet and juicy and provides fiber, which perhaps I need right now. No more nasty surprises occurred that day but I noticed with glum displeasure less food in my dinner dish and the treats noticeably absent.

A couple of weeks later I was back to my normal svelte and Aireodynamic self. Well almost. Except for my paws which were itchy, so much so they drove me crazy and I found myself obsessively licking and chewing them. *Not again.* I thought I was over the itchy stuff. I had at last graduated to some real food and dreaded the thought I would have to go back to the tasteless mush I ate for so long, and with admirable grace I might add. Always something it seemed.

I had heard people say that this part of the country is hard on dogs and I think I am perhaps beginning to understand why. I tried not to be discouraged that I suffered from more problems than most of my pals. I knew no humans could be better dog pawrents than mine so I shrugged it off as the luck of the draw and tried my best to put up my best front.

Anna helped. She took to wiping my paws with soothing little damp squares every time I came in. She also inspected the inside of my pads for those prickly burrs that sometimes got jabbed deep between the them, a move I hated but I resigned myself to the necessity of being coddled. So much for being superdog and living up to my tough heritage. *Sigh.* I had suffered problems of one type or another since puppyhood but I didn't dwell on them. Dogs live in the present, which is the best way I think, so I soldiered through and continued on, loving life, always eager for the next adventure.

Aire attack

TODAY ANNA HAD TO push me to get up, unusual for my normal bouncy self but I was so very comfy. "C'mon sleepyhead, up and at 'em."

Wait, whah? The nerve. Anyone with any sense knows you don't wake a sleeping Airedale. She's lucky I didn't get my growl on.

This wasn't Anna's first rodeo. She knew how to do it. She wafted a piece of cheese under my nose. The aroma produced the desired effect and I woke up enough to search for the source.

What in the world made Anna so chirpy at this time of the morning I wondered? To be fair, she gave me time to open my eyes and stretch, then grab my breakfast, but almost before I finished I found myself leashed up and out the door.

Okay, I'm always up for a walk and it was a fine day, just a touch of chill and sunny with a frisky breeze. Still not fully awake I ambled about stopping every few steps to sniff the wind and retrieve messages, of which there were plenty. There were so many I was forced to make my replies short but I didn't mind.

We reached the community garden in our own sweet time with me using my directional scan on full alert. As a result, halfway along the trail my laser-focused eyesight picked up something new. Not wanting to take away from Anna's fun in discovering something furst, I pretended not to notice until she said "Alf, look at this, a stick library."

What did she mean a stick library? I saw a bunch of the things piled up against a sign but can't say it excited me much.

"You can take one but before you leave you must put one back. What a great idea." Anna was clearly entranced.

Me, not so much. As a king among terriers, such mundane things as sticks were beneath me. *What would I do with a stick?* Anna knows this. *What is going on with her today?*

"Alf, sometimes I think I should have got a poodle," she groused. "No interest at all? Look at Ollie. He's picking up sticks and returning them."

Hmph. Ollie is the next door neighbor's dog, a retriever so, of course he would be obsessive about sticks. Retriever's are strange that way. He is an okay guy, a bit older than me and not much into romping around anymore. We didn't cross paths often.

Now he pranced along, full of himself, toting yet another stick back to the rack. The way he carried on he must have appointed himself the branch manager *hee hee*. I acknowledged him in passing but didn't stop. I was not impressed.

"You've got quite the attitude today young fella." Anna said, seeming a little put out with my lack of enthusiasm.

Poodle, schnoodle. Did you know if you let a Poodle's hair grow it turns into dreadlocks? How would you like that then? Wait. What? Attitude? Me? Seriously? Who knew? How long have I lived with you guys? Have you forgotten yourself today Anna? I'm an AIREDALE. We're born with attitude. You know that. I stood up and stalked off forcing Anna to head back to the trail.

After checking some interesting messages I relaxed again and got into the zone, greeting all the dogs and their humans along the way. Maybe Anna had the right idea, it really was a beautiful day. *Wait, what is that?* I bent down to investigate hoping to discover a sleeping squirrel. No such luck, but an intriguing critter. Four short legs stuck out from a hard-looking shell and a head on a long neck with beady eyes stared up at me. As soon as it caught me looking, it pulled its head back until it disappeared inside the shell. *Cool.* I lunged closer to to take a look.

"Be careful Alf." Anna said. "That's a gopher tortoise. He's a big one isn't he? You can have a whiff of him but go easy, no pawing, scratching or biting."

Anna could be a real killjoy sometimes but I got it and after a thorough sniff all over I backed off, pleased to see the tortoise poke his head out again and start to amble off on his way wherever.

I was still staring at him when I heard this series of furious little war shrieks that sounded like a cat with a tonsil problem and a brown blob raced at me from across the street in a blur of fur. I stopped, planting all four paws and stared, wondering if I was being attacked by a gerbil, but no, this tiny bundle of hair, which stood straight up all over like a rock star shocked by his guitar, turned out to be a micro me and a girl at that.

She barreled into me at warp speed, a tornado with teeth, yipping and biting along the way, apparently with every intention of killing me. Mortified I did nothing for a moment. I had never been attacked by a girl, though last year a wee guy tried it on before his embarrassed owner restrained him. *Why*, I wondered? All the girls I knew adored me. *Was this one off her rocker? She did look like she might be short a brain cell or two.*

As that thought passed I looked down to find my paw hurting and the little beast's sharp tiny fangs buried in it. I lifted it up out of her reach, or so I thought, but no, she did not let go so I sat with my paw in the air beseeching Anna with a pained expression. I am a gentleman. I could not harm a girl, least of all one this small. It was beyond embarrassing.

Anna, however found herself otherwise occupied. The short, extremely plump owner of this tiny monster dropped her leash in surprise when what she thought was her darling little

Yorkie turned in a second into a snarling attack wolf, for no apparent reason I could think of.

As the tiny brat (you wouldn't be off the mark if you took the B off that word, *hee hee*) raced towards me, her stubby owner puffed and waddled behind her evidently terrified I would dispatch her little darling and eat her for dinner, if her horrified expression and red face were anything to go by.

Waddling seemed to be a rare form of exercise for this female and her hair stood out like her little beast's in protest. Anna ran around me trying to grab the tiny pink leash, one of those that shot out from a handle when a button was pushed and trapped unsuspecting people around the legs leaving, in some cases, horrible wounds.

I still sat with my paw in the air watching this fiasco play out. It actually hurt quite a lot, though I wouldn't admit it. The girl sported teeth like a raptor, unimaginable in such a small body, but I maintained my pose of kingly dignity. I would never live down the shame of admitting to injury from this little beast. It would have been comical if it happened to someone else, but it didn't, it happened to me. *Oh the shame.*

We waited, frozen in place until the little she devil's owner puffed up, full of apologies. Anna, obviously wanting to say a lot more than she did, made our excuses, pried the mutt's teeth from my paw and started back for home. I stalked away with what I considered admirable hauter but once we rounded the corner I admit to playing for sympathy by pretending a painful limp. Of course it didn't work. Anna examined my paw and knew there was no real damage. Maybe not to my paw, but a whole lot to my ego. I lowered my eyebrows and took a sneaky glance around, relieved no one appeared to witness the attack of a king by a midget.

I wondered if the little female was part bulldog and would have never released me if she hadn't been forced to do so. That's what happens when you get up too early.

As expected, Anna told the story to Harry who chortled and asked me "What happened to that old mantra - Airedales don't start fights, they finish them?" He dubbed it 'The gerbil incident' and proceeded to remind me of it every chance he got. Harry should remember that Airedales don't get mad, they get even. I admit my ego was a bit bruised and Harry's enjoyment in taunting me sent my day further into the blue funk mode but I perked myself up by remembering I had, in fact, acted with admirable restraint; and also in plotting my revenge.

Aire cooled

THE WEATHER TURNED unseasonably cold for our part of the world and stayed that way for a couple of weeks, a novelty for us southerners. I reveled in it. We Airedales love cold weather. The colder the better. We get all frisky and bound around with glee. The humans not so much. They started looking a little out of sorts and began sneezing and coughing all over the place. I offered love and nose pokes. *What is wrong with you guys?* I tried licks and nips which weren't received well. Affronted I backed off to regroup.

Apart from my meals I was left to my own devices as my poor pawrents suffered a miserable condition. I wanted to try my best to help. After all they looked after me when I got sick. *What to do*? I wish they spoke fluent Dale. Why are people so dense? Worried, I wormed my way in between them as they huddled on the sofa and lay down trying to offer comfort. The best thing I could do seemed to be staying quiet, not a cinch for me. I did my best, keeping one eye on them and my ears pricked ready for any intruder disturbing the peace. It turned out they both had colds. Do dogs catch colds? Yes we can, with the same symptoms as people but as you know colds are a virus so it is unlikely we would catch one from people and I didn't.

Life got even more weird and I struggled to understand why it was everybody walked about wearing muzzles now. *Did they bite somebody? Why are the parks empty? Why don't we go to visit my lady friends or my favorite humans anymore?* My pawrents got over their colds but now they stay at home all the time. It was fun at first but now its just booooring. They were even doing it at the vet when I went for my regular checkup. My people stayed in the car and the vet helpers came outside to fetch me, all wearing muzzles and dresses with their hands covered. I didn't want to go in there. I never wanted to go in any more. I visited the doc way too often and wearied of being pricked and poked. I sensed their worry and that scared me more than anything. I was relieved to be returned to my family and not kept in that place for some other awful procedure.

It took some time, but in the end I adjusted to the new reality though I didn't understand it and I was despondent our world had shrunk so small. Even when we went out we stayed some distance from everyone else we met. That made it almost impossible to greet other dogs but, being chipper by nature, I made the best of the situation, hoping this nonsense would not go on too long. Little did I know. The world had gone bananas and showed no signs of returning to normal.

Airebrushed

HARRY GOT UP ONE day in a grumpier mood than I had ever seen him. He is finicky about his hair which had grown quite long and shaggy. He had more hair than most males around his age. It had never occurred to me before but now I realized Harry had to get groomed too. I guessed he couldn't do that with this new lifestyle we were all dealing with.

Anna got a little testy with him complaining about it but he rendered her speechless when he said she should cut his hair for him.

"Not a chance. I don't know anything about cutting hair. You'll end up looking like a big hedgehog or worse, and I know how picky you are about your haircuts. I'll never hear the end of it." Anna shook her head. "No and no. No way. Absolutely not."

Guess who won? Beaten down by grumbles, Anna spent a few hours watching TV shows of people cutting hair and then one morning she walked out into the cage room and with a fancy wave indicated the chair next to her. Harry gave her a suspicious look but sat down and Anna wrapped a towel around his front with a flourish. I watched with glee. Someone else was getting groomed. *Hee hee.*

Harry held up a mirror and squinted every which way to be sure Anna did what he wanted. I think she wanted to cut off more than his hair, *woofles*, and I was having a grand time. I planted myself in front of Harry to make sure I didn't miss anything. At that moment I really wished I spoke human. I had a lot to say and I had not forgotten Harry was due a payback or two.

For the fun of it I gazed at Harry, tilting my head at different angles while he stared at me, hopefully making him think Anna was doing something that he wasn't going to like. I think it worked because a worried expression settled on his face. Unable to contain myself I stood and paced around a bit and then did a couple of spins before sitting back down and giving Harry a nudge. He didn't say anything but the look he skewered me with could freeze dog biscuit. Didn't faze me, of course. When she finished we both agreed Anna had done a fine job. I think she was surprised herself, as well as relieved. She still gripped the scissors in her hand when she turned to look at me with a speculative frown. *Oh oh, time to make myself scarce.*

I stayed alert, trying to delay the inevitable but if Harry thought his hair was a bit shaggy he wasn't a patch on me and it didn't take long for Anna to corner me with the dreaded grooming tools. It turned out that appointing Anna my personal stylist was much better than the people who did that for money. She only insisted on working for a few minutes at a time. No standing on a grooming table for hours, and she brought me a thing called a lick mat. She spreads peanut butter on it and that keeps me so engrossed I don't take notice of any humiliations she is inflicting on me while I eat.

She's pretty sneaky is Anna and I have to say I felt much better without all that hair weighing me down. I wouldn't pass muster at Westminster but I did still look like an Airedale. Not bad for an amateur and much more enjoyable.

Dire times

ONE GOOD THING that happened cheered me up a bit. Some men arrived on the lot across the water with rackety machines which banged and screeched with ear popping noises as they rumbled around clearing the land. I felt sorry for the animals they evicted and now had to find a new home but I was excited to find I could now scan a much bigger area. The men left not so much as a stick to block my view. Now I could bark at those fishermen people who dared to trespass too close to my Aireland and bark I did.

Once, another dog showed up with them and he barked at me. *What fun.* His voice coming over the water sounded like it came through one of those horn things people used. It reached much farther than normal so I knew that mine, going the other way did the same thing. People would think me a muscled monster like a dire wolf, and be properly terrified. Those guys had to be a scary size, dire wolves. They coexisted with the saber-toothed cats, fearsome beasts. Everything was bigger back then. The dire wolf had a special yen for horses, bison, even mastodons. Not like us canines who are omnivores.

One reason the dire wolves went extinct, according to the egghead humans, is because the vegetation changed and prey became much smaller. Poor guys had trouble catching small prey and by then the grey wolf had muscled in. He was much better at catching smaller dinners.

Another reason is because the dire wolf was not a wolf. No, poor thing, not even a canine. He was, in fact, a separate species whose nearest relative might have been the jackal. Poor thing was unable to mate with us canids and that spelled his doom.

I rambled again didn't I? Finished conversing with the other pooch and powerless to make the fishermen heed my warnings I sat back and watched as the men threw nets into the water and pulled up a bunch of fish. I did not approve of them poaching our water creatures and hoped the fish in our pond knew how lucky they were to be protected by the cage, and me. I greeted them every morning to be sure everyone was okay. The fish these guys hauled up reminded me of a story Harry told about fish that escaped from farms in an island south of us, Cuba he called it. Somehow they arrived here and could survive for three days out of the water. Yes. African walking catfish he called them and said they could eat puppies. *Yowls*. I would be sure to give any fish shuffling along on land a wide berth.

Aire horn

AND THEN IT HAPPENED again, another health hitch. When would it end? This time I had been burning off energy happily racing around my back yard. It felt so amazing, the freedom to blow off steam and in celebration I jumped for a low hanging branch of a nearby bush, not my best decision. I twisted and landed awkwardly to immediate agony in my leg. Hobbling on the other three I made my way back into the house.

The folks, used to my klutziness, and unfazed by it, left me alone to rest, unaware something more serious was going on, but when it became obvious I was still in severe pain it was off to see the wizard, *of dogs that is,* again. I began to think I should have my own private apartment in the place with my name on it. The girls took me inside and I went through all the tests and picture taking before being deposited back in the car. The way things were done now Anna didn't actually see the vet man face to face and she found this frustrating, but rules were rules.

He called her phone and she turned it up loud so Harry, and I, could hear what he had to say. It wasn't good. The doc said this was the same knee I injured last year but this time it was worse and he called my injury these complicated doctor terms - cruciate ligament tear and I picked up the words 'surgery and long recovery'. I didn't like the sound of that. Harry and Anna grew somber and the doc kept talking. Any time he does that I know I'm not going to like it.

I think of his building now as the house of misery, but I always let them take me inside and I stay on my best behavior with everyone so why do they do such awful things to me? One time I saw some humans crying and their fur-kid lying on the floor. I knew he was dead. Someone else came in and closed the door. I know this is a place that tries to help us because the folks often mention it but sometimes I wonder if they have been given the wrong advice. I don't understand but I trust my family. Once in a while I have some dreadful pain when I'm there and I let them know to back off. When that happens I conk out and have no idea what went on after my warning until I wake up. *Huh.*

Things did not improve when I got home. The doc gave me a shot and sent the pawrents home with medicine so the pain got much better but other things are getting worse. Harry built me a cage in the living room with my bed in it. He made sure it is very spacious, but it is still a cage. *What for?*

"It's okay Alf. Its just so you don't run around too much and jump on the furniture. You mustn't do that for a while so you don't hurt yourself more, okay?"

I didn't like it, but the drugs made me sleepy and the cushions were comfy so I didn't object. I'm not allowed to go so much as a step without my leash now, not even my back yard. *What is going on? Am I ever going to see my cousins again?* Anna helps me spend some time by teaching me new things and she bought some new toys. Love my snuffle mat. Another one she bought is not worth my time. I'm supposed to find hidden treats but its no challenge for an Airedale. She does try.

The folks discussed my upcoming surgery. Due to the new rules at the vet clinic no one was allowed inside, and they felt reluctant to set this up. As usual when something like this comes up, Anna retreated to her trusty computer box and read everything she could find and then some, about my condition. As a result, they opted to wait. Eavesdropping on this conversation I heard how this operation involved cutting out bones, *drools and shakes*. That sounded horrific to me. No way would that happen. I wouldn't let it.

I let out the breath I'd been holding with a whoosh when I heard about the reprieve. Instead, I had to continue staying in my cage and submit to having my leash attached every time I left it and I had to do that for at least a month. This was much better, even with the pain. Since I didn't feel so hot it turned out this was not hard at first and slowly I began to feel more my normal self.

None of my pals could come to play, which saddened me but the good news is that Anna threw away that awful food and I got back on the tasty stuff as well as my regular treats and some super yummy ones for being such a good sport. In that respect things were looking up.

Then, a pack leader belonging to one of my cousins sent Anna and me to this lady who lived in the next town. She's a vet but more involved in rehab than normal vet care, which I took to mean getting better a more natural way, *yea*, than most of them. She fitted me with a pair of goggles and settled me down on a big blanket next to a small machine. Not anxious to experience the unknown I balked a bit, wary of this new turn of events but she was kind and gentle and Anna sat next to me so I figured it wouldn't be too bad.

It wasn't. She ran the wand thing on the end of the machine over my leg for a few minutes and that was that. Getting ready to go she told Anna I would only need one more session of this thing, laser she called it and as I got better she would give me some exercises to do. It turns out animal doctors aren't taught much about working with muscle injuries. Who'd have thunk it?

As time passed Anna and I went on short leash walks and car rides. Harry helped me climb in when we went out on these occasions and I appreciated the change of scenery. Over time the walks got longer and I did not hurt or limp. We went back to the lady vet a couple of times and she demonstrated some exercises for me to do to strengthen my leg. She also helped me balance on a big blue ball, scary at first but it soon became fun. I wished this lady vet lived closer to us, I liked her a lot. We did all the exercises as we were told and I felt myself getting better.

Then one day Anna came to my cage smiling nonstop. "It's been a month now Alf, the doc says everything looks good. He is amazed and told me this does not happen often. Perhaps the injury was not as serious as they thought. Whatever the case, you are one lucky guy. We can get back to normal as your leg has healed, but no craziness," she told me. Next time you might re-injure this knee more easily."

Yea. We took things slowly. Harry took down my cage and allowed me the freedom of the house again. After a few days of that and Anna watching me like a hawk they let me out in the back yard without a leash. As the days passed it became evident I was indeed fully healed and could run and play without risk. I don't know why, whether my bone picture had been misread or they were being overly cautious, or I am just plain lucky. It doesn't matter. I recovered from a serious condition, thanks in great part to my family. Perhaps now I could recover from all my other pesky problems. The tide was turning.

Back once more to my normal rambunctious self, trials and tribulations forgotten, I missed the visits to the other members of my tribe until one day my ears pricked up at one of Anna's endless phone calls.

When she held this little box to her ears it always seemed like she talked to herself which puzzled me for a long time but today I heard the magic words "terrier walk." We all attended this event every year and I yipped and spun, ecstatic to hear it would take place as promised, even if all the people had to be muzzled again. *Yea*. Anna was pleased because this event took place away from any town and we would all walk, leashed, on a long meandering trail before sitting down at an outdoor restaurant for lunch.

I found it next to impossible not to bounce around in my excitement. I think even the folks had trouble because they had been housebound for so long. The prospect of an outdoor meet with friends was just as exciting to them as it was to me. The drive took forever but the traffic was minimal and we made it on time.

We met in a barking lot and barking there was as about forty terriers of all breeds scrambled to say their hellos along with their humans. Once that was sorted, we started off trekking in twos or threes and soon entered a tree-lined leafy trail. The trees on both sides bent toward each other and formed an archway, blocking out the sun.

There were a zillion new things to check out and about halfway along, the trail branched into a clearing where most everyone was unleashed to run around, not me of course, but I understood.

One little guy stood out with a character much bigger than his size. He zoomed all over the place at an awe- inspiring pace on those short little legs and with much joy, raced in to chivvy the others and then out again to dash to the end of the clearing. He looked exactly like me only much smaller. No, he wasn't a Welsh Terrier but a Lakeland. Not a breed seen much in this part of the world. I envied his drive and spunk but on the QT, was grateful at being restrained because the walk had done me in.

When the other dogs wore themselves out we headed back by a different route and once at the restaurant, I sank down next to Anna's chair for a rest, only raising my head when I realized the odds of a choice titbit coming my way were on my side. The humans had all worn their muzzles but the eating place was outside, under a fancy tent and tables were spaced some distance apart so they were able to unmask, so to speak, and enjoy their food. Even the weather had been perfect, a terrierific day. It really was, Fox terriers, Welsh terriers, Jack Russells, a Border or two, even a Sealyham, and the Lakeland. A diverse representation of all our kind.

Home once more we all settled in for a lazy evening. I looked forward to my soft, inviting bed, so much that I retired just after dinner and was snoozing away when my pawrents called it a night. We all thought it would be a good night's sleep but after only a few hours of rest Harry and Anna jerked up in bed like they had been shot, disturbing my beauty sleep.

"Was that Alf?" Harry asked. "It sounded like an Aireraid? I have never heard a howl so loud. It almost took the roof off and was downright scary, worse than that Gator roar we heard once, do you remember?"

Huh? What? I opened one eye, the other still being asleep.

Anna stared at me in horror. "Alf, wake up. What's wrong? Are you in pain? Did you have a nightmare? You scared the stuffing out of us. I have never heard you do anything like that." She climbed out of bed to check me over.

Awake now, but my brain not yet functioning, I sat up and looked around with lidded eyes. Let me tell you, it is never a good idea to wake up a sleeping dog, definitely not one who is howling, but I had already been deprived of sleep by all the fuss, so it wasn't so bad.

I directed a quizzical look at my disheveled and bleary-eyed humans. Anna checked me out, in none too gentle detail, and proclaiming herself satisfied I was not in imminent danger, went back to bed shaking her head. So now I feel the need to tell you about sleeping dogs, for your own safety. Listen up.

We dogs have similar sleep cycles to people and as with people, it is good for our memory. The brain gathers together different bits of information into memory. That is why, if you tried to teach us something during the day it will be better in the morning, usually that is, *hee hee*. Taking a snooze can improve our performance.

As far as dreams go, we are likely dreaming of you, which can be pleasing or annoying, *hee hee*. We associate everything we come into contact with to a feeling. It's how we know the people we like. You've seen that, right? A dog that doesn't like a certain person, that's how we do it.

Events are generalized into feelings so if we have a restless night emotions are affecting our sleep and yes we can have PTSD and emotional pain. Rescue dogs remember the experiences they went through and likely howling in their sleep is a nightmare from their traumas. In my case, I may well have had a nightmare, or grief for a lost friend may have surfaced in my dream, or maybe a response to a noise.

Dogs also howl in their sleep when they are lonely or in distress. Perhaps I howled because my subconscious sensed something momentous coming. I was fast asleep so I didn't know why I howled but I was super chuffed to know it was an excellent one. Yesterday, Anna showed me a picture of the biggest rabbit I had ever seen on her picture machine. I looked at it, astounded. Whoever knew a rabbit that size existed? She said it was a Flemish Giant Rabbit weighing in at twenty pounds. What a catch that would be, so yes, I might well have been dreaming of a bunny monster. My family, having never heard me do that before were awestruck at the volume of sound that erupted into their peaceful night. Thrilled with my performance I closed my eyes and drifted back into dreamland.

A bridge too far

THE NEXT FEW DAYS found me enjoying the Spring weather, but not overdoing it. I took life easy, not really thinking about it but well aware that another looming birthday meant a natural slowdown. After all, we dogs age much faster than humans. Also I was now used to the slower pace of life and staying at home most of the time due to the strange sickness that worried all the humans.

I didn't mind the lack of exercise, preferring to stay with Anna as she puttered around the house. This contentment had me stretching like a cat. I think we all enjoyed the relaxed period of being a close little family. Even Harry mellowed, spending a lot of time tinkering around his car room. Just to be fair, I joined him sometimes though I preferred the coziness of the house now. We all relished these good lazy days.

Then, one morning, I was a bit slow waking up to find that Anna had decided to give me a trim. Resigned to it, I submitted without protest, probably because I felt a little bit yucky. It started when I went outside to do my business. Being an Airedale, I ignored the discomfort and tried to be my normal cheerful self but the feeling got worse.

Anna started my trim and I didn't want to worry her so I sat still and tried to enjoy the gentle brushing she was giving me. It worked for a while until everything slowed down and I couldn't suppress a quiet whimper, petrified by the weird sensations running through me. I didn't know what was happening, but I had the glimmer of an idea.

Anna responded at once. "Sorry Alf. You need a break eh?" She let me loose. "Go take a break then while I clean up all this hair."

I gave her a nose poke in thanks and wobbled out to the dining room, some instinct telling me to go outside, but just before reaching the door the bad sensation became monstrous. I fell down and to my horror my bladder let loose. From a long distance I heard Anna rushing over to help me. She reached my side and knelt down just as everything went black.

———————————————

Hello everyone. My name is Archie and it is with some trepidation I introduce myself to you here in Alf's diary. What you say, where's Alf and why hasn't he written in so long? Is he still sick?

The portion you have just read is several years old (other than the last paragraph) and was his last. That is why it has been such a long time since you heard from him. Sadly, I have to bring you the terrible news.

In his last few months, Alf's visits to the vet became more and more frequent. He fought his way through one health problem after another as well as suffering with a bum ticker.

He was the runt of his litter and smaller than his siblings. Not sure if that caused his bad heart which led to all the other problems but he never complained, lived his life full of joy and mischief without complaint, a true trooper and worthy of being called a King of Terriers.

Anna stopped the Diary and she and Harry spent their time caring for him, trying to keep a good quality of life going, and for the most part they did. Along the way they dealt with that pandemic thing, hurricanes, life complications, etc. You guys know all about that I'm sure.

Alf slowed down some more but still enjoyed his life until one day four years ago he walked into the living room, lay down and died. Anna and Harry were devastated but glad for Alf that his crossing to the rainbow bridge was quick and painless. His heart just gave up and stopped.

He was a guy with a big heart and left a huge hole in his pawrents lives. Their hearts hurt for so long they struggled to climb out from the cloud of grief, but eventually they grew to realize only another fur-kid could fill the hollow space that descended on their lives because, as you know, when we dogs pass on, we take a chunk of your hearts with us.

Along came me. I have huge paws to fill and I know it will take time. I cannot replace the paw tracks Alf left on your hearts but I would be so happy to add to those tracks with my own if you would let me. I wish I could have met Alf. I feel like I did because pictures of him are everywhere, Airelooms, but the next best thing for me is to take care of the humans he left behind. I humbly hope you will give me the chance to pick up where Alf left off. So here's my story.

I was born in the land of yankees, a prince among princes, I was told, as my half brother was a champion show dog and I was meant to follow in his pawsteps. The spare you might say. I did in fact, for a while spending the furst two human years of my life in this way, living in a kennel with occasional outings to the ring and watching my brothers and sisters leave for other homes. Don't get me wrong. It was a happy time. I was well looked after and got to spend time running in the fields with my sisters, I had no idea things were about to change.

My owners decided one day that my brother was doing so well they needed to concentrate their time with him and so, to my horror, I became just another surplus mouth to feed. They searched for someone else to give me a home and two people came to meet me one day. I am a confident and social guy so I greeted them politely and with enthusiasm having no idea why they came. Next thing I know I found myself bundled in a crate and driven halfway across the country.

I couldn't fathom why my family no longer wanted me. After all, I was two, not a puppy. I assumed my home was my home for life. The abruptness of my departure left me distraught, confused and terrified. Me, who had never yet experienced heartbreak. I was so devastated by this betrayal I stood up for the entire journey staring behind me at everything familiar I had ever known that now was gone from my life. I had been abandoned, thrown away without so much as a goodbye. How could people do that?

By the time we arrived at our destination I was none the wiser. These people did not stop or speak to me throughout the whole journey. I was not able to get a sense of them. I had no idea where we were or what would become of me now but I am an Airedale and I met these new circumstance as best I could. When we stopped in this strange place my head felt as if it was on a swivel as I stared around looking for the kennels, but all I saw was one building behind a stretch of grass. The humans led me in there.

I had never been inside a house before. These people did not take me around or let me explore. Over the next few days I had to learn it was not acceptable to potty in this building. When I did, accustomed to doing my business wherever I wanted, they got furious and yelled and smacked me. I didn't know why. I had never been smacked before. I crept into a corner, reluctant to get near them again, confused and miserable.

I had never seen a television screen or heard a vacuum cleaner. I didn't know what to do, how to act to make them happy or where to sleep. The female was alright, but the man was horrible. Every time I did something wrong he came at me with a hairbrush. It didn't take very long before I decided to go home.

Whenever the door opened I dashed for it and raced off as fast as I could. *How could my wonderful people have abandoned me to live with these mean and awful humans?* I thought all people were kind and affectionate. It was a hard lesson to learn that they were not, but I am an Airedale. I will always remember that. I will not stay here.

After the third or fourth escape attempt, they had enough, locked me in their car again and returned to my home. Thank you Dog.

Life returned to normal again except I no longer went into the show ring. That was okay by me, more time to play with the ladies. After a while the trauma receded and I got back to my normal self. A few months later the big RV pulled up the driveway and I anticipated my brother would be off to another show but this time they loaded me up too. I wasn't worried, as this was normal for our road trips.

We traveled to yet another town and the next morning I was let into a small enclosure near the RV while my brother was prepped and fussed over for another show. The fresh air was nice but I was getting bored sitting in a barking lot with not much of interest around to distract me, until that is, two new humans rounded the corner and were greeted by my folks. I love people so I perked up and ran to meet the strangers.

I barely had time to swallow the cheese they offered before I found myself led to an unfamiliar wagon and loaded into a crate. *Oh no*. They were getting rid of me again. *How could they do this?*

The strangers climbed in the front and the car took off. Grief stricken, I once again watched as everything familiar receded into the distance. Remembering the last time, I started to shake and drool, unable to believe I had done something so wrong that my family didn't care what became of me, only that they were rid of me.

The lady in the front reached back to stroke me gently, offering soothing words and treats. I ignored her, afraid now to trust strangers or to think about where they were taking me and what awful change would now be in my life.

My life with Anna and Harry had begun but that's another story. I hope you will let me tell it.

ABOUT THE AUTHOR:

P.J. Erickson is the author of five previous novels and a member of the National Writers Association. She is the willing sidekick of her fourth Airedale, Remington. In between adventures with him and transcribing Alf's dictation, she enjoys life in the Sunshine State. She loves chocolate, hates housework and sailing and is driven to write.

Contact her at pj@embarqmail.com.

Made in the USA
Columbia, SC
24 January 2024

30868641R00112